The Writing of the Disaster

L'Ecriture du désastre

by Maurice Blanchot

translated by Ann Smock

New Edition

University of Nebraska Press
Lincoln and London

First paperback printing
of the new edition: 1995

An index has been added
to the New Edition.

Contents

Translator's Remarks   *vii*

The Writing of the Disaster   *1*

Index   *151*

Translator's Remarks

I have encountered two kinds of difficulty in translating this book. First, there is the kind posed by the fact that, here more than in previous works, Blanchot lets thoughts suggest themselves and develop, through puns, alliterations, rhymes, etymologies (both learned and fanciful), as though thought were engraved in words themselves and thinking consisted in deciphering the inscription, or as if language were speaking to us in the various sonorities of diverse terms, and we had only to listen to what it tells — in short, as if he believed language to be the reserve and preserve of truth ("language, the house of being"). Irony, to be sure, does not fail him with respect to this faith in language (irony is an important word, and effect, in *The Writing of the Disaster*). Indeed, as though he had only to read out the lesson in irony from the words of his own language, he says of trust in language (*confiance*) that it is *défiance* — distrust, nay defiance. Defiance *of* language, situated *in* language, which finds within itself the terms of its own critique. Or, he attributes the "crypticness" of language — its way of concealing and conserving meaning — to the crypts within it, the recesses where inside is out and thus cannot be brought out (where the secret, all exposed, cannot be discovered). Such effects (*confiance-défiance*, or *cryptique-crypte-indécryptable*) are often hard to reproduce. Sometimes I have had recourse to a footnote or to a snatch of the original between brackets in the body of the text.

The second kind of difficulty I want to mention (often, of course, the two kinds are intertwined) comes up when the expression in question is a proper name, or has a cognate in English, or is a perfectly ordinary expression whose equally ordinary equivalent in English comes to mind automatically. Examples: *le multiple, le désastre, l'écriture du désastre,* "Auschwitz," *le silence.* For though you can write down "the multiple," "the disaster," and so on, with *some* assurance, you have to learn from the whole book what these words could possibly mean, or what it could possibly mean that they be written. The following remarks are intended to suggest what I have come to understand by a few of the English words that I have written down here. I choose these few because each seems to me "key."

(*"The translation is infinite. And yet it is necessary that we find the key word that opens and does not open."*)

1. Readers of *Death Sentence*[1] might associate "the disaster" with the title of that narrative: with the ultimatum that bears upon the ultimate, the stop put to the coming of that stop. "I call disaster," Blanchot says, "that which does not have the ultimate for a limit, but bears the ultimate away in the disaster."

2. "The writing of the disaster" is one among several similar expressions: "the thought of the disaster," for example, "knowledge of the disaster," and also "the flight of thought," the interruption of the incessant." Of this last expression Blanchot comments that "interruption" and "incessant" mean the same thing. Such sameness is among the obsessions of this book, and it is the same as this obsession: "the Other."

Blanchot stresses the reversibility of all expressions of the type "the ———— of ————," adding that they cannot be turned around. He writes: "Desire of writing, writing of desire. Desire of knowledge, knowledge of desire. Let us not believe that we have said anything at all with these reversals." Such expressions have a motionless instability. They reverse, turn back, re-turn without cease, but as though it were ceaselessly that they reached a point of no return. "The interruption of the incessant" does not *simply* mean an intervention arresting the heretofore continuous; it also means the interruption that the incessant introduces—the break which the uninterrupted, the unbroken, is. The break in what? In interruption, in the very possibility of a break? Such an interruption—but none, on account of this interruption, is possible—is "the interruption of the incessant."

Similarly: "the writing of the disaster" means not simply the process whereby something called the disaster is written—communicated, attested to, or prophesied. It also means the writing done by the disaster—by the disaster that ruins books and wrecks language. "The writing of the disaster" means the writing that the disaster—which liquidates writing—is, just as "knowledge of the disaster" means knowledge *as* disaster, and "the flight of thought" the loss of thought, which thinking is.

What *happens* to knowledge when, disastrously for the very possibility of knowledge, and indeed for the possibility of *this* knowledge, it becomes knowledge of the disaster? One answer is: *nothing*. For the disaster that befalls knowledge when it is knowledge of the disaster prevents it or, you might say, saves it from being this knowledge, this disaster (knowledge of the disaster). "The disaster takes care of everything," Blanchot says.

The writing of the disaster: the erasure of whatever it is that by this writing is written, the effacement of lines that cannot have been drawn if not by the stroke that now deletes them.[2] "When to write or not to write makes no difference, then writing changes; it is the writing of the disaster." That there should be no difference (no difx

ference as difference is ordinarily understood) between disaster and none at all: this is the disaster. That there should be no change: this is the change, the "radical change" (*changement radical*).

That there should be no break between life and death: this is dying, *le mourir*, stronger than death, stronger than *la mort*. Nothing is so strong: the *irony* of it is *disastrous* for all systems — linguistic, philosophical, political. Also it is called weakness, human weakness, *la faiblesse humaine*. But not in order to deny that the methods of the mighty should be employed against them.

3. This "is" the disaster: that there neither is, nor is not, disaster. Neither, nor: the "neutral" (*le neutre*), which means "outside" the whole which, together, the one term and the other (being and not-being) comprise. "Outside" (*hors*): foreign to the union of the one and the other, to communion, to community. The French word brings to mind several expressions: *hors-la-loi* ("outlaw"), for example, but also *hors série, hors ligne, hors pair*. These designate the exceptional. Here "exceptional" means not so much superior or inferior to the norm as exempt from that distinction; without regard for the opposition normal-abnormal; dismissed by the structures which, differentiation by differentiation, smoothly account for all. The "space" that Blanchot calls "the outside" (*le dehors*), is outside the difference inside-outside. In the same way, the disaster is outside being *and* not-being — presence and absence, consciousness and unconsciousness. "Detachment" is a word related to "outside," and it is defined as detachment from everything, including detachment. Such detachedness characterizes the "fragmentary" writing of the disaster.[3]

"Outside. Neutral. Disaster. Return." These are the names of four winds, Blanchot says at one point, four winds that blow from nowhere through this book. Return: inasmuch as it befalls its own befalling, the disaster never does befall. Never once, but ever once again. It repeats, but not anything; it is the recurrence of no occurrence (it is "outside" the realm of phenomena, of experience — "*hors phénomène, hors expérience,"* Blanchot says); it is not anything's return, but return "itself."

4. You might say it is the return of the time there is not—the first time, the last time, the "one and only time" of the disaster which, occurring, obliterates occurrence. This "absence of time" is the undepletable intervening time between the disaster and that very catastrophe which, long past when it occurs, has still to happen when nothing can happen anymore. Blanchot calls this interval, between *no longer* and *not yet*—this endless wait for the time already exhausted—the lapse of time (*le laps du temps*) or the interim (*le délai*). Or, sometimes, the immediate (*l'immédiat*).

The word "scene," though ill-suited because it tends to suggest something spectacular, lends itself well enough to evoking what "happens" in the interim, in that at least it allows one not to speak as though of something taking place in time, Blanchot says. And indeed, the following question introduces the text which it is hard not to think of as the center of *The Writing of the Disaster*: "(A primal scene?)" Whoever wishes to be on the lookout for the "central concerns" of this book, and the links among them, might anticipate relations between this "scene," the rather extended discussions of the child in Winnicott's and Serge Leclaire's thoughts, and of the child-god Narcissus, and the passages that name the event in history that consumed all history in its flames, the holocaust.

5. The infinitive often indicates the *timelessness* of the interim, the measurelessness of the abyss between the arrival of the disaster, say, and the arrival of the disaster. A particularly insistent use of the infinitive is *dire* ("to say, tell, speak"), quite often capitalized and employed as a substantive (*le Dire*). This expression evokes Emmanuel Levinas and his conviction that speech alone sustains the relation of a subject to the Other. Speech: not any particular communication, but speech itself as an offering, the offering of language in response to the infinite obligation which the presence

to me of an other person is. In Blanchot, the infinitive (*le Dire*) reminds us not to confuse the element in which the human relation persists—reminds us not to confuse the Word—with anything said, anything spoken, just as the (disastrous) abyss between the disaster and . . . the disaster reminds us not to confuse the relation—of the "one" to the "other"—with anything that is. Or, that is not.

Readers of other Blanchot texts (*The Space of Literature*, for example)[4] will recognize in *le Dire* the language no one speaks, the language not of me or of you or of any*one*, but of language. In this sheer reiteration, or semblance of language—the other of language and the language of the other—nothing is said. (Nor is anything kept silent: silence speaks, nothing is said.) It seems that *le Dire* is similar to return, the return of no occurrence, as distinct from something (or any*one*) returning. For *le Dire* is speaking, sheer telling, as distinct from anything told (or kept secret). With *le Dire* and *le retour* I believe I am right to connect *le multiple* (especially in the expression *le multiple comme multiple*) and also *la différence*, when Blanchot explicitly sets it apart from *le différent*. By *le différent* I take him to mean something that is different from some other thing, or difference when it is the difference between one thing and another. *La différence*, however (which may be sensed between the arrival of the disaster and the arrival of the disaster), isn't the difference there is, between one thing and another; it is all the difference there isn't: not just a rift in the same—a break in the continuous, "the interruption of the incessant"—but very sameness *as* an immeasurable rift ("the interruption of the incessant").

"The multiple *as* multiple," Blanchot says at one point, introduces us to "the *Als Struktur*," which rules out any multiple at one with itself, or any difference which is the same as it is: that is, any multiple which *isn't* unity, any difference which isn't sameness. "The multiple as multiple" means the multiple as one, and the one as one (or "the One," *L'Un*) means the one as multiple. The one, the multiple; difference, sameness; the self, the other: misnomers for what cannot be named but surrenders indifferently to the one (improper name) or to the other. The other.

The other *as* other, in the devastating weight of the responsibility "I" bear for him. "The other is neither the one nor the other," Blanchot wrote in *L'Entretien infini.*[5] Neither the one nor the other: the neutral.

6. I have translated *Dire* and *le Dire* as "Speaking," "Telling," or "Saying," proceeding as though there were a word in French that would have the relation to *dire* that *l'écriture* ("writing") has to *écrire* ("to write"). Or rather I have learned that *l'écriture* does not, precisely, have to *écrire* the relation of *le dit* to *dire*, but rather, the relation of *le dire* to *dire*. *Ecriture* is the word in French, not for what is written, but for what otherwise would have to be called *l'Ecrire*.

It isn't the word for what is written (Blanchot never uses the term *l'écrit*) but seems, rather, the word for what is to be, for what remains to be (*ce qui reste*). *Ecriture* seems to designate what is left still to say when everything that can be has been — the remains of that which is always already completely over. *L'écriture du désastre.*

Bartleby the scrivener appears intermittently in these pages as one to whom the appellation "writer" is "a-propriate"; he does not do anything, he prefers not to. Writing: doing, when nothing is to be done, when nothing is being done. Neither activity nor passivity, but the action of passiveness. "Passion" names this feverish urgency of patience, and "patience" this cold stillness of passion. In these words ("passive," "passion," "patience"), the "not" (*pas*) that recurs is also a *pas* ("step"). Notice it here, too: "passage." It "is" a step over the edge, beyond the point of no return, that changes everything (including change), and that is not ever once taken, but is always taken, over again. Obsessively it repeats, like the step of the other, to whom more than everything is owed, at my door; like knowledge of the disaster (disaster as knowledge, knowledge as disaster) — like the final wish of all who suffered the death camps: "Know what has happened, do not forget, and at the same time never will you know."

The Writing of the Disaster

♦ The disaster ruins everything, all the while leaving everything intact. It does not touch anyone in particular; "I" am not threatened by it, but spared, left aside. It is in this way that I am threatened; it is in this way that the disaster threatens in me that which is exterior to me—an other than I who passively become other. There is no reaching the disaster. Out of reach is he whom it threatens, whether from afar or close up, it is impossible to say: the infiniteness of the threat has in some way broken every limit. We are on the edge of disaster without being able to situate it in the future: it is rather always already past, and yet we are on the edge or under the threat, all formulations which would imply the future—that which is yet to come—if the disaster were not that which does not come, that which has put a stop to every arrival. To think the disaster (if this is possible, and it is not possible inasmuch as we suspect that the disaster is thought) is to have no longer any future in which to think it.

The disaster is separate; that which is most separate.

When the disaster comes upon us, it does not come. The disaster is its imminence, but since the future, as we conceive of it in the order of lived time, belongs to the disaster, the disaster has always already withdrawn or dissuaded it; there is no future for the disaster, just as there is no time or space for its accomplishment.

♦ *He does not believe in the disaster. One cannot believe in it, whether one lives or dies. Commensurate with it there is no faith, and at the same time a sort of disinterest, detached from the disaster. Night; white, sleepless night—such is the disaster: the night lacking darkness, but brightened by no light.*

♦ The circle, uncurled along a straight line rigorously prolonged, reforms a circle eternally bereft of a center.

♦ "False" unity, the simulacrum of unity, compromises it better than any direct challenge, which, in any case, is impossible.

♦ Would writing be to become, in the book, legible for everyone, and indecipherable for oneself? (Hasn't Jabès almost told us this?)

♦ If disaster means being separated from the star (if it means the decline which characterizes disorientation when the link with fortune from on high is cut), then it indicates a fall beneath disastrous necessity. Would law be the disaster? The supreme or extreme law, that is: the excessiveness of uncodifiable law—that to which we are destined without being party to it. The disaster is not our affair and has no regard for us; it is the heedless unlimited; it cannot be measured in terms of failure or as pure and simple loss.

Nothing suffices to the disaster; this means that just as it is foreign to the ruinous purity of destruction, so the idea of totality cannot delimit it. If all things were reached by it and destroyed—all gods and men returned to absence—and if nothing were substituted for everything, it would still be too much and too little. The disaster is not of capital importance. Perhaps it renders death vain. It does not superimpose itself upon dying's scope for withdrawal, filling in the void. Dying sometimes gives us (wrongly, no doubt), not the feeling of abandoning ourselves to the disaster, but the feeling that if we were to die, we would escape it. Whence the illusion that suicide liberates (but consciousness of the illusion does not dissipate it or allow us to avoid it). The disaster, whose blackness should be attenuated—through emphasis—exposes us to a certain idea of passivity. We are passive with respect to the disaster, but the disaster is perhaps passivity, and thus past, always past, even in the past, out of date.

♦ *The disaster takes care of everything.*

♦ The disaster: not thought gone mad; not even, perhaps, thought considered as the steady bearer of its madness.

♦ The disaster, depriving us of that refuge which is the thought of death, dissuading us from the catastrophic or the tragic, dissolving our interest in will and in all internal movement, does not allow us to entertain this question either: what have you done to gain knowledge of the disaster?

♦ The disaster is related to forgetfulness—forgetfulness without memory, the motionless retreat of what has not been treated—the immemorial, perhaps. To remember forgetfully: again, the outside.

♦ "Have you suffered for knowledge's sake?" This is asked of us by Nietzsche, on the condition that we not misunderstand the word "suffering": it means, not so much what we undergo, as that which goes under. [1] It denotes the *pas* ["not"] of the utterly passive, withdrawn from all sight, from all knowing. Unless it be the case that knowledge—because it is not knowledge of the disaster, but knowledge as disaster and knowledge disastrously—carries us, carries us off, deports us (whom it smites and nonetheless leaves untouched), straight to ignorance, and puts us face to face with ignorance of the unknown so that we forget, endlessly.

♦ The disaster: stress upon minutiae, sovereignty of the accidental. This causes us to acknowledge that forgetfulness is not negative or that the negative does not come after affirmation (affirmation negated), but exists in relation to the most ancient, to what would

4

seem to come from furthest back in time immemorial without ever having been given.

♦ It is true that, with respect to the disaster, one dies too late. But this does not dissuade us from dying; it invites us—escaping the time where it is always too late—to endure inopportune death, with no relation to anything save the disaster as return.

♦ Never disappointed, not for lack of disappointment, but because of disappointment's always being insufficient.

♦ I will not say that the disaster is absolute; on the contrary, it disorients the absolute. It comes and goes, errant disarray, and yet with the imperceptible but intense suddenness of the outside, as an irresistible or unforeseen resolve which would come to us from beyond the confines of decision.

♦ To read, to write, the way one lives under the surveillance of the disaster: exposed to the passivity that is outside passion. The heightening of forgetfulness.

It is not you who will speak; let the disaster speak in you, even if it be by your forgetfulness or silence.

♦ The disaster has already passed beyond danger, even when we are under the threat of ————. The mark of the disaster is that one is never at that mark except when one is under its threat and, being so, past danger.

♦ To think would be to name (to call) the disaster the way one reserves, in the back of one's mind, an unspoken thought.

I do not know how I arrived at this, but it may be that in so doing I struck upon the thought which leads one to keep one's distance from thought; for it gives that: distance. But to go to the end of thought (in the form of this thought of the end, of the edge): is this not possible only by changing to another thought? Whence this injunction: do not change your thought, repeat it, if you can.

◆ The disaster is the gift; it gives disaster: as if it took no account of being or not-being. It is not advent (which is proper to what comes to pass): it does not happen. And thus I cannot ever happen upon this thought, except without knowing, without appropriating any knowledge. Or again, is it the advent of what does not happen, of what would come without arriving, outside being, and as though by drifting away? The posthumous disaster?

◆ Not to think: that, without restraint, excessively, in the panicky flight of thought.

◆ *He said to himself: you shall not kill yourself, your suicide precedes you. Or: he dies inept at dying.*

◆ Limitless space where a sun would attest not to the day, but to the night delivered of stars, multiple night.

◆ *"Know what rhythm holds men."* (Archilochus.) Rhythm or language. Prometheus: *"In this rhythm, I am caught."* Changing configuration. What is rhythm? The danger of rhythm's enigma.

◆ *"Unless there should exist, in the mind of whoever dreamed up humans, nothing except an exact count of the pure rhythmical motifs of being, which are its recognizable signs."* (Mallarmé.)

◆ The disaster is not somber, it would liberate us from everything if it could just have a relation with someone; we would know it in light of language and at the twilight of a language with a *gai savoir*. But the disaster is unknown; it is the unknown name for that in thought itself which dissuades us from thinking of it, leaving us, but its proximity, alone. Alone, and thus exposed to the thought of the disaster which disrupts solitude and overflows every variety of thought, as the intense, silent and disastrous affirmation of the outside.

◆ A nonreligious repetition, neither mournful nor nostalgic, a return not desired. Wouldn't the disaster be, then, the repetition—

the affirmation—of the singularity of the extreme? The disaster or the unverifiable, the improper.

♦ There is no solitude if it does not disrupt solitude, the better to expose the solitary to the multiple outside.

♦ Immobile forgetfulness (memory of the immemorable): so would the disaster without desolation be de-scribed, in the passivity of a letting-go which does not renounce, does not announce anything if not the undue return. Perhaps we know the disaster by other, perhaps joyful names, reciting all words one by one, as if there could be for words an all.

♦ *The calm, the burn of the holocaust, the annihilation of noon—the calm of the disaster.*

♦ He is not excluded, but like someone who would no longer enter anywhere.

♦ Penetrated by passive gentleness, he has, thus, something like a presentiment—remembrance of the disaster which would be the gentlest want of foresight. We are not contemporaries of the disaster: that is its difference, and this difference is its fraternal threat. The disaster would be in addition, in excess, an excess which is marked only as impure loss.

♦ Inasmuch as the disaster is thought, it is nondisastrous thought, thought of the outside. We have no access to the outside, but the outside has always already touched us in the head, for it is the precipitous.

The disaster, that which disestablishes itself—disestablishment without destruction's penalty. The disaster comes back; it would always be the disaster after the disaster—a silent, harmless return whereby it dissimulates itself. Dissimulation, effect of disaster.

♦ *"But there is, in my view, no grandeur except in gentleness."* (S. W.)[2] I will say rather: nothing extreme except through gentleness. Madness through excess of gentleness, gentle madness.

To think, to be effaced: the disaster of gentleness.

◆ *"There is no explosion except a book."* (Mallarmé.)

◆ The disaster, unexperienced. It is what escapes the very possibility of experience—it is the limit of writing. This must be repeated: the disaster de-scribes. Which does not mean that the disaster, as the force of writing, is excluded from it, is beyond the pale of writing or extratextual.

◆ *It is dark disaster that brings the light.*

◆ The horror—the honor—of the name, which always threatens to become a title.[3] In vain the movement of anonymity remonstrates with this supernumerary appellation—this fact of being identified, unified, fixed, arrested in the present. The commentator says (be it to criticize or to praise): this is what you are, what you think; and thus the thought of writing—the ever-dissuaded thought which disaster awaits—is made explicit in the name; it receives a title and is ennobled thereby; indeed, it is as if saved—and yet, given up. It is surrendered to praise or to criticism (these amount to the same): it is, in other words, promised to a life surpassing death, survival. Boneyard of names, heads never empty.

◆ The fragmentary promises not instability (the opposite of fixity) so much as disarray, confusion.

◆ Schleiermacher: By producing a work, I renounce the idea of my producing and formulating myself; I fulfill myself in something exterior and inscribe myself in the anonymous continuity of humanity—whence the relation between the work of art and the encounter with death: in both cases, we approach a perilous threshold, a crucial point where we are abruptly *turned back.* Likewise, Friedrich Schlegel on the aspiration to dissolve in death: "The human is everywhere the highest, even higher than the divine." The human movement is the one that goes right to the limit. Still, it is possible that, as soon as we write, and however little we write (the little is only too much), we know we are approaching the limit—the perilous threshold—the chance of being turned back.

For Novalis, the mind is not agitation, disquietude, but repose (the neutral point without any contradictions). It is weight, heaviness. For God is "an infinitely compact metal, the heaviest and most bodily of all beings." "The artist in immortality" must work at reaching the zero where soul and body become mutually insensitive. "Apathy" was Sade's term.

♦ Lassitude before words is also the desire for words separated from each other—with their power, which is meaning, broken, and their composition too, which is syntax or the system's continuity (provided the system be in some way complete in advance and the present a *fait accompli*). This lassitude, this desire is the madness which is never current, but the interval of unreason, the "he'll have gone mad by tomorrow"—madness which one mustn't use to elevate, or to deepen, or to lighten thought with it.

♦ Garrulous prose: a child's mere babble. And yet a man who drools, the idiot, the man of tears who restrains himself no longer, who lets himself go—he too is without words, bereft of power, but still he is closer to speech that flows and flows away than to writing which restrains itself, even if this be restraint beyond mastery. In this sense, there is no silence if not written: broken reserve, a deep cut in the possibility of any cut at all.

♦ Power in the broadest sense—capacity, ability—is like the power of the group leader: always related to domination. *Macht* is the means, the machine, the functioning of the possible. The delirious and desiring machine tries, in vain, to make disfunction function. In vain, for un-power is not delirious; it has always departed from the groove already, and is always already derailed; it belongs to the outside. It does not suffice to say (in order to speak of un-power): power can be held provided it not be used. For such abstinence is the definition of divinity. Detachment is not sufficient, unless it senses that it is, in advance, a sign of the disaster. The disaster alone holds mastery at a distance. I wish (for example) for a psychoanalyst to whom a sign would come, from the disaster. Power over the imaginary provided that the imaginary be understood as that which evades power. Repetition as un-power.

◆ We constantly *need* to say (to think): that was quite something (something quite important) that happened to me. By which we mean at the same time: that couldn't possibly belong to the order of things which come to pass, or which are important, but is rather among the things which export and deport. Repetition.

◆ Among certain "primitive" peoples (those whose society knows no State), the chief must prove his dominion over words: silence is forbidden him. Yet it is not required that anyone listen to him. Indeed, no one pays attention to the chief's word, or rather all feign inattention; and he, in fact, says nothing, but repeats the celebration of the traditional norms of life. To what requirement of primitive society does this empty language, which emanates from the apparent locus of power, answer? The discourse of the chief is empty precisely because he is separated from power—it is the society itself which is the locus of power. The chief must move in the element of the word, which is to say, at the opposite pole from violence. The chief's obligation to speak—that constant flow of empty speech (not empty, but traditional, sheer transmission), which he *owes* to the tribe—is the infinite debt which effectively rules out speaking man's ever becoming a man of power.

◆ There is a question and yet no doubt; there is a question, but no desire for an answer; there is a question, and nothing that can be said, but just this nothing, to say. This is a query, a probe that surpasses the very possibility of questions.

♦ He who criticizes or thrusts the game away, has already entered into the game.

♦ How can anyone claim: "What you by no means know can by no means torment you?" I am not the center of what I know not, and torment has its own knowledge to cover my ignorance.

♦ Desire: let everything be more than everything, and still be all.

♦ There can be this point, at least, to writing: to wear out errors. Speaking propagates, disseminates them by fostering belief in some truth.

To read: not to write; to write what one is forbidden to read.

To write: to refuse to write—to write by way of this refusal. So it is that when he is asked for a few words, this alone suffices for a kind of exclusion to be decreed, as though he were being obliged to survive, to lend himself to life in order to continue dying.

To write—for lack of the wherewithal to do so.

♦ Inconsolable solitude. The motionless disaster which nevertheless approaches.

♦ How could there be a *duty* to live? The more serious question: the desire to die, too strong, it seems, to be satisfied with *my* death, and to be exhausted when I die, is, paradoxically, the desire that others might live without life's being for them an obligation. The desire to die absolves of the duty to live—that is, its effect is that one lives without any obligation (but not without responsibility, for responsibility is beyond life).

♦ Reading is anguish, and this is because any text, however important, or amusing, or interesting it may be (and the more engaging it seems to be), is empty—at bottom it doesn't exist; you have to cross an abyss, and if you do not jump, you do not comprehend.

♦ Wittgenstein's "mysticism," aside from his faith in unity, must come from his believing that one can *show* when one cannot *speak*.

But without language, nothing can be shown. And to be silent is still to speak. Silence is impossible. That is why we desire it. Writing (or Telling, as distinct from anything written or told) precedes every phenomenon, every manifestation or show: all appearing.

◆ Not to write — what a long way there is to go before arriving at that point, and it is never sure; it is never either a recompense or a punishment. One must just write, in uncertainty and in necessity. Not writing is among the effects of writing; it is something like a sign of passivity, a means of expression at grief's disposal. How many efforts are required in order not to write — in order that, writing, I not write, in spite of everything. And finally I cease writing, in an ultimate moment of concession — not in despair, but as if this were the unhoped for: the favor the disaster grants. Unsatisfied and unsatisfiable desire, yet by no means negative. There is nothing negative in "not to write"; it is intensity without mastery, without sovereignty, the obsessiveness of the utterly passive.

◆ To fail without fail: this is a sign of passivity.

◆ To want to write: what an absurdity. Writing is the decay of the will, just as it is the loss of power, and the fall of the regular fall of the beat, the disaster again.

◆ Not to write: negligence, carelessness do not suffice; the intensity of a desire beyond sovereignty, perhaps — a relation of submersion with the outside, passivity which permits one to keep in the disaster's fellowship.
He devotes all his energy to not writing, so that, writing, he should write out of failure, in failure's intensity.

◆ Unmanifest anguish. Were you in anguish, you wouldn't be.

◆ The disaster is what one cannot welcome except as the imminence that gratifies, the wait for un-power.

◆ May words cease to be arms; means of action, means of salvation. Let us count, rather, on disarray.

When to write, or not to write makes no difference, then writing changes — whether it happens or not; it is the writing of the disaster.

◆ Let us not entrust ourselves to failure. That would only be to indulge nostalgia for success.

◆ Beyond seriousness there is play, but beyond play, and seeking that which out-plays (the way the disaster de-scribes), there is the gratuitous, from which no escape. It is what by chance befalls, and I fall beneath it, having always fallen already.

Days and nights go by in silence. Such is the word.

◆ Detached from everything, including detachment.

◆ One of the ruses of the self: to sacrifice the empirical self the better to preserve a transcendental or formal I; to annihilate oneself in order to save one's soul (or knowledge, including un-knowledge).

◆ Not writing should not refer back to some "not wanting to write," nor — although this is more ambiguous — to an "I cannot write," which in fact still indicates, in a nostalgic way, the relation of an I to power, in the form of power's loss. But not writing without any reference to power: this supposes that one go by way of writing.

◆ Where is there the least power? In speech, or in writing? When I live, or when I die? Or again, when dying doesn't let me die?

◆ Is it an ethical concern that distances you from power? Power links, un-power detaches. Sometimes un-power is sustained by the intensity of the undesirable.

◆ Bereft of certitude, he does not doubt; he hasn't that support.

◆ The thought of the disaster, if it does not extinguish thought, makes us insouciant with regard to the results this thought itself can have in our life; it dismisses all ideas of failure and success; it replaces ordinary silence—where speech lacks—with a separate silence, set apart, where it is the other who, keeping still, announces himself.

♦ Withdrawal and not expansion. Such would be art, in the manner of the God of Isaac Louria, who creates solely by excluding himself.

♦ Writing is evidently without importance, it is not important to write. It is from this point that the relation to writing is decided.

♦ The question concerning the disaster is a part of the disaster: it is not an interrogation, but a prayer, an entreaty, a call for help. The disaster appeals to the disaster that the idea of salvation, of redemption might not yet be affirmed, and might, drifting debris, sustain fear.

The disaster: inopportune.

♦ It is the other who exposes me to "unity," causing me to believe in an irreplaceable singularity, for I feel I must not fail him; and at the same time he withdraws me from what would make me unique: I am not indispensable; in me anyone at all is called by the other— anyone at all as the one who owes him aid. The un-unique, always the substitute. The other is, for his part too, always other, lending himself, however, to unity; he is neither this one nor that one, and nonetheless it is to him alone that, each time, I owe everything, including the loss of myself.

The responsibility with which I am charged is not mine, and because of it I am no longer myself.

♦ "Be patient." A simple motto, very demanding. Patience has already withdrawn me not only from the will in me, but from my power to be patient: if I *can* be patient, then patience has not worn out in me that me to which I cling for self-preservation. Patience opens me entirely, all the way to a passivity which is the *pas* ["not"] in the utterly passive, and which has therefore abandoned the level of life where *passive* would simply be the opposite of *active*. In this way we fall outside inertia; the inert thing which submits without reacting, becomes as foreign as its corollary, vital spontaneity, purely autonomous activity. "Be patient." Who says this? No one who can say it, and no one who can hear it. Patience can neither be advised nor commanded: it is the passivity of dying whereby an I that is no longer I, answers to the limitlessness of the disaster, to that which no present remembers.

◆ Through patience, I take upon myself the relation to the Other of the disaster— the relation which does not allow me to assume it, or even to remain myself in order to undergo it. Through patience, all rapport between myself and a patient self is broken.

◆ From the moment when the imminent silence of the immemorial disaster caused him, anonymous and bereft of self, to become lost in the other night where, precisely, oppressive night (the empty, the ever dispersed and fragmented, the foreign night) separated him and separated him so that the relation with the other night besieged him with its absence, its infinite distantness— from that moment on, the passion of patience, the passivity of a time without present (absent time, time's absence), had to be his sole identity, circumscribed by a temporary singularity.

◆ If there is a relation between writing and passivity, it is because both presuppose the effacement, the extenuation of the subject: both presuppose a change in time, and that between being and not-being, something which never yet takes place happens nonetheless, as having long since already happened. The uneventfulness of the neutral wherein the lines not traced retreat;[4] the silent rupture of the fragmentary.

◆ Passivity: we can evoke it only in a language that reverses itself. I have, at other times, referred to suffering: suffering such that I could not suffer it. If I had recourse to the thought of such suffering, it was so that in this un-power, the I excluded from mastery and from its status as subject (as first person)—the I destitute even of obligation—could lose itself as a self capable of undergoing suffering. There is suffering, there would be suffering, but no longer any "I" suffering, and this suffering does not make itself known in the present; it is not borne into the present (still less is it experienced in the present). It is without present, just as it is without beginning or end; time has radically changed its meaning and its flow. Time without present, I without I: this is not anything of which one could say that experience—a form of knowledge—would either reveal or conceal it.

But the word "suffering" is too ambiguous. The ambiguity will never be dispelled, for, speaking of passivity, we cause it to appear, if only in the night where dispersion marks it, deleting all sign of it. It is very difficult for us—and thus all the more important—to speak of passivity, for it does not belong to the world, and we know nothing which would be utterly passive (if we did, we would inevitably transform it). Passivity, the contrary of activity: such is the ever-restricted field of our reflections. We might coin a word for the absolute passiveness of total abjection—*le subissement,* which is [patterned on *subir,* "to undergo," but is also] simply a variation of *subitement* ["suddenly"], or the same word crushed; we might invent that term, *le subissement,* in an attempt to name the inert immobility of certain states said to be psychotic, the *patior* in passion, servile obedience, the nocturnal receptivity of mystics—dispossession, that is, the self wrested from itself, the detachment whereby one is detached from detachment, or again the fall (neither chosen nor accepted) outside the self. Still, these situations, even if some are at the limit of the knowable and designate a hidden face of humanity, speak to us hardly at all of what we seek to understand by letting this characterless word be pronounced, *passivity.*

◆ There is the passivity which is passive quietude (suggested, perhaps, by what we know of quietism); and then there is the passivity which is beyond disquietude, but which nevertheless retains the passiveness of the incessant, feverish, even-uneven movement of error which has no purpose, no end, no starting principle.

◆ The discourse on passivity necessarily betrays passivity, but it can effectively indicate certain of the traits that cause its faithlessness: not only is discourse active; it unfolds and develops according to the rules that assure it a certain coherence. Not only is it synthetic, conforming to a certain unity of language and to a time which, always the memory of itself, maintains itself in a synchronic whole. To be sure, activity, development, coherence, presence of a whole— none of these characteristics are characteristic of passivity. But there is more to the infidelity: the discourse on passivity makes passivity appear. It presents and represents passivity, whereas passivity is, perhaps (perhaps), that "inhuman" part of man which, destitute of power, separated from unity, could never accommodate anything able to appear or show itself. This part of man makes no sign or indication of itself and thus, through dispersion and defection, always falls short of what can be stated, even provisionally, about it.

So it is that if we feel bound to say something about passivity, it is because passivity matters to man without moving him over into the realm of things that matter—and also because, escaping our power to speak of it as well as our power to test it (to try or experience it), passivity is posed or deposed as that which would interrupt our reason, our speech, our experience.

◆ This is what is strange: passivity is never passive enough. It is in this respect that one can speak of an infinite passivity: perhaps only because passivity evades all formulations—yet it seems that there is in passivity something like a demand that would require it to fall always short of itself. There is in passivity not passivity, but its demand, a movement of the past toward the insurpassable.

Passivity, passion, past, *pas* (both negation and step—the trace or movement of an advance): this semantic play provides us with a slippage of meaning, but not with anything to which we could entrust ourselves, not with anything like an answer that would satisfy us.

◆ Refusal is said to be the first degree of passivity. But if refusal is deliberate and voluntary, if it expresses a decision — though this be a negative one — it does not yet allow separation from the power of consciousness, and comes no closer to passivity than this act, of refusal, on the part of a self. And yet refusal does tend toward the absolute, independent of any determination whatsoever. This is the core of refusal which Bartleby the scrivener's inexorable "I would prefer not to" expresses: an abstention which has never had to be decided upon, which precedes all decisions and which is not so much a denial as, more than that, an abdication. Bartleby gives up (not that he ever pronounces, or clarifies this renunciation) ever saying anything; he gives up the authority to speak. This is abnegation understood as the abandonment of the self, a relinquishment of identity, refusal which does not cleave to refusal but opens to failure, to the loss of being, to thought. "I will not do it" would still have signified an energetic determination, calling forth an equally energetic contradiction. "I would prefer not to . . . " belongs to the infiniteness of patience; no dialectical intervention can take hold of such passivity. We have fallen out of being, outside where, immobile, proceeding with a slow and even step, destroyed men come and go.

◆ Passivity is measureless: for it exceeds being; it is being when being is worn down past the nub — the passivity of a past which has never been, come back again. It is the disaster defined — hinted at — not as an event of the past, but as the immemorial past (*Le Très-Haut*) which returns, dispersing by its return the present, where, ghostly, it would be experienced as a return.

◆ Passivity. We can evoke situations of passivity: affliction; the final, crushing force of the totalitarian State, with its camps; the servitude of the slave bereft of a master, fallen beneath need; or dying, as forgetfulness of death. In all these cases we recognize, even though it be with a falsifying, approximating knowledge, common traits: anonymity, loss of self; loss of all sovereignty but also of all subordination; utter uprootedness, exile, the impossibility of presence, dispersion (separation).

♦ In the relation of the self (the same) to the Other,[5] the Other is distant, he is the stranger; but if I reverse this relation, the Other relates to me as if I were the Other and thus causes me to take leave of my identity. Pressing until he crushes me, he withdraws me, by the pressure of the very near, from the privilege of the first person. When thus I am wrested from myself, there remains a passivity bereft of self (sheer alterity, the other without unity). There remains the unsubjected, or the patient.

♦ In the patience of passivity, I am he whom anyone at all can replace, the nonindispensable by definition, but one for whom nonetheless there is no dispensation: he must answer to and for what he is not. His is a borrowed, happenstance singularity—that, in fact, of the *hostage* (as Levinas says). The hostage is the nonconsenting, the unchosen guarantee of a promise he hasn't made, the irreplaceable one who is not in his own place. It is through the other that I am the same, through the other that I am myself: it is through the other who has always withdrawn me from myself. The Other, if he calls upon me, calls upon someone who is not I: the first come or the least of men; by no means the unique being I would like to be. It is thus that he assigns me to passivity, addressing himself in me to dying itself.

(The responsibility with which I am charged is not mine and causes me not to be I.)

♦ If, in the patience of passivity, my self takes leave of me in such a way that in this outside—where being lacks without giving place to not-being—the time of patience (time of time's absence, or time returning never present, the time of dying) has no more support, no longer finding anyone to sustain it, then by what language other than fragmentary — other than the language of shattering, of infinite dispersal — can time be marked, without this mark's making it present and pointing it out to the authority which assigns names? But the fragmentary, of which there is no experience, also escapes us. Silence does not take its place; scarcely even does reticence — the reticence of that which can no longer keep still, not knowing, anymore, how to speak.

◆ The death of the Other: a double death, for the Other is death already, and weighs upon me like an obsession with death.

◆ In the relation of *myself to the Other,* the Other exceeds my grasp. The Other: the Separate, the Most-High which escapes my power — the powerless, therefore; the stranger, dispossessed. But, in the relation of *the Other to me,* everything seems to reverse itself: the distant becomes the close-by, this proximity becomes the obsession that afflicts me, that weighs down upon me, that separates me from myself — as if separation (which measured the transcendence from me to the Other) did its work within me, dis-identifying me, abandoning me to passivity, leaving me without any initiative and bereft of present. And then, the other becomes rather the Overlord, indeed the Persecutor, he who overwhelms, encumbers, undoes me, he who puts me in his debt no less than he attacks me by making me answer for his crimes, by charging me with measureless responsibility which cannot be mine since it extends all the way to "substitution." So it is that, from this point of view, the relation of the Other to me would tend to appear as sadomasochistic, if it did not cause us to fall prematurely out of the world — the one region where "normal" and "anomaly" have meaning.

And yet because the other, according to Levinas's designation, replaces the Same, just as the Same substitutes for the Other, it is henceforth in me — a me without selfhood — that the signs of transcendence (of a transcendence) appear. Whence this high contradiction, this highly significant paradox: when passivity idles and destroys me, I am at the same time pressed into a responsibility which not only exceeds me, but which I cannot exercise, since I cannot do anything and no longer exist as myself. Such responsible passivity would be *Speaking.* For before anything is spoken, and outside of being (*inside,* there is passivity and there is activity, opposed and complementary; there is inertia and dynamism, involuntary and voluntary), Speaking gives and gives the response, answering to the impossible and for the impossible.

But there is an ambiguity which the paradox does not eliminate. If I, bereft of selfhood, withstand (not that I could be said even to have experienced it) this passive passivity when the other crushes me into radical alienation, is my relation still a relation to the other? Is it not rather a relation to the "I" of the master, to absolute egotistical force, to the dominator who predominates and ultimately wields the force of inquisitorial persecution? In other words, I must answer for the persecution that opens me to the longest patience and which is in me the anonymous passion, not only by taking it upon myself regardless of my own consent; I must also answer to it with refusal, resistance, and combat. I must come back to knowledge; I must return (if possible—for it may be that there is no return) to the I that knows and that knows it is exposed, not to the Other, but to the adverse I, to egotistical Omnipotence, to murderous Will. Naturally, this Will draws me thereby into its game and makes me its accomplice, but that is why there must always be at least two languages, or two requirements: one dialectical, the other not; one where negativity is the task, the other where the neutral remains apart, cut off both from being and from not-being. In the same way each of us ought both to be a free and speaking subject, and to disappear as passive, patient—the patient whom dying traverses and who does not show himself.

◆ Weakness is grief weeping without tears; it is the murmur of the plaintive voice or the restless rustling of that which speaks without words, the dearth, the exhaustion of appearance. Weakness eludes all violence, which, even if it is oppressive omnipotence, can do nothing to the passivity of dying.

♦ It is upon losing what we have to say that we speak—upon an imminent and immemorial disaster—just as we say nothing except insofar as we can convey in advance that we take it back, by a sort of prolepsis, not so as finally to say nothing, but so that speaking might not stop at the word—the word which is, or is to be, spoken, or taken back. We speak suggesting that something not being said is speaking: the loss of what we were to say; weeping when tears have long since gone dry; the surrender which the invisible passivity of dying announces but does not accomplish—*human weakness.*

♦ That the other has no meaning except the infinite aid which I owe him—that he should be the unlimited call for help to which none but I can answer—does not make me irreplaceable; still less does it make me unique. But it causes me to disappear in the infinite movement of service where I am only temporarily singular and a simulacrum of unity. I cannot draw any justification (either for my worth as a stand-in or for my being) from a demand that is not addressed to anyone in particular, that demands nothing of my determination and that in any case exceeds me to such a degree that it disindividualizes me.

♦ The interruption of the incessant: this is the distinguishing characteristic of fragmentary writing: interruption's having somehow the same meaning as that which does not cease. Both are effects of passivity. Where power does not reign—nor initiative, nor the cutting edge of a decision—there, dying is living. There dying is the passivity of life—of life escaped from itself and confounded with the disaster of a time without present which we endure by waiting, by awaiting a misfortune which is not still to come, but which has always already come upon us and which cannot be present. In this sense, the future and the past come to the same, since both are without present. So it is that men who are destroyed (destroyed without destruction) are as though incapable of appearing, and invisible even when one sees them. And if they speak, it is with the voice of others, a voice always other than theirs which somehow accuses them, interrogates and obliges them to answer for a silent affliction which they bear without awareness.

♦ It is as though he said: "May happiness come for all, provided that by this wish, I be excluded from it."

♦ If the Other is not my enemy (as he is sometimes in Hegel — albeit a benevolent one — and especially in the early philosophical writings of Sartre), then how can he become the one who wrests me from my identity and whose proximity (for he is my neighbor) wounds, exhausts, and hounds me, tormenting me so that I am bereft of my selfhood and so that this torment, this lassitude which leaves me destitute becomes my responsibility? For responsibility is the extreme of *subissement*: it is that for which I must answer when I am without any answer and without any self save a borrowed, a simulated self, or the "stand-in" for identity: the mandatory proxy. Responsibility is innocent guilt, the blow always long since received which makes me all the more sensitive to all blows.[6] It is the trauma of creation or of birth. If the creature is "he whose situation is ceded to him by the other," then I am created responsible. My responsibility is anterior to my birth just as it is exterior to my consent, to my liberty. I am born thanks to a favor which turns out to be a predestination — born unto the grief of the other, which is the grief of all. The Other, Levinas says, is encumbering. But is this not once more the Sartrian perspective — the nausea that we get not from the lack but from the excess of being? Is the other not a surplus of which I would like to divest myself, but toward which I cannot possibly be unconcerned, since it is the other who obliges me to take his place even in indifference, and to be no more than his stand-in?

♦ Here, perhaps, is an answer. If the Other calls me into question to the point of stripping me of myself, it is because he is himself absolute nakedness, the entreaty [*supplication*] which disqualifies the me in me till it becomes sheer torture [*supplice*].

◆ The unrelated (in the sense that the one [I][7] and the other cannot be as one, or come together at one and the same time—cannot be contemporaries) is initially the other for me. Then it is I as other from myself. It is that in me which does not coincide with me—my eternal absence, that which no consciousness can grasp, which has neither effect nor efficacy and is passive time. It is the dying which, though unsharable, I have in common with all.

◆ I cannot welcome the Other, not even with an acceptance that would be infinite. Such is the new and difficult feature of the plot. The other, as neighbor, is the relation that I cannot sustain, and whose approach is death itself, the mortal proximity (he who sees God dies: for "dying" is one manner of seeing the invisible, of saying the ineffable. Dying is the indiscretion wherein God, become somehow and necessarily a god without truth, surrenders to passivity).

◆ If I cannot welcome the Other by answering the summons which his approach exerts to the point of exhausting me utterly, it is surely through awkward *weakness* alone (through the wretched "after all, despite everything," and through my portion of derision and folly) that I am called upon to enter into this separate, this other relation. I am called to enter it with my selfhood gangrened and eaten away, altogether alienated (thus it is among lepers and beggars beneath the Roman ramparts that the Jews of the first centuries expected to discover the Messiah).

◆ As long as the other is distant (the face that comes from the absolutely far away and bears the mark of distantness, the trace of eternity, of the immemorial past), then only the relation to which the other, whose face it is, assigns me, in the wake of absence, is *beyond* being. Only this relation, and not selfhood or identity. (Levinas writes: "Beyond being is a Third person who is not defined by selfhood.") But when the other is no longer the remote, but the neighbor whose proximity weighs upon me to the point of opening me to the radical passivity of the self, then subjectivity—subjectivity as wounded, blamed, and persecuted exposure, as vulnerability abandoned to difference—falls in its turn outside of being. Then it signifies the beyond of being, in the very gift—in the giving of the sign—which its immeasurable sacrifice delivers to the other. Then subjectivity, in the same capacity as the other and as the face, is the enigma which troubles order and breaks with being: it is the exemption of the extraordinary, exclusion from the domain of that which can appear, exile from the realm of experience.

◆ Passivity and inquiry: passivity lies, perhaps, at the end of inquiry; but is it still within reach of any question? Can the disaster be interrogated? Where might one find the language in which answer, question, affirmation, negation may well intervene, but without any effect? Where is the speaking—as distinct from anything that can be spoken—which eludes every mark, the mark of foretelling and likewise of forbidding?

◆ When Levinas defines language as contact, he defines it as immediacy, and this has grave consequences. For immediacy is absolute presence—which undermines and overturns everything. Immediacy is the infinite, neither close nor distant, and no longer the desired or demanded, but violent abduction—the ravishment of mystical fusion. Immediacy not only rules out all mediation; it is the infiniteness of a presence such that it can no longer be spoken of, for the relation itself, be it ethical or ontological, has burned up all at once in a night bereft of darkness. In this night there are no longer any terms, there is no longer a relation, no longer a beyond—in this night God himself has annulled himself.

Or, one must manage somehow to understand the immediate in the past tense. This renders the paradox practically unbearable. Only in accordance with such a paradox can we speak of disaster. We can no more think of the immediate than we can think of an absolutely passive past, but patience in us vis-à-vis a forgotten affliction is the mark of this past, its oblivious prolongation. When we are patient, it is always with respect to an infinite affliction which does not reach us in the present, but befalls by linking us to a past without memory. Others' affliction, and the other as affliction.

◆ Responsibility: a banal word, a notion moralistically assigned to us as a (political) duty. We ought to try to understand the word as it has been opened up and renewed by Levinas so that it has come to signify (beyond the realm of meaning) the responsibility of an other philosophy (which, however, remains in many respects eternal philosophy).[8] Responsible: this word generally qualifies—in a prosaic, bourgeois manner—a mature, lucid, conscientious man, who acts with circumspection, who takes into account all elements of a given situation, calculates and decides. The word "responsible" qualifies the successful man of action. But now responsibility—my responsibility for the other, for everyone, without reciprocity—is displaced. No longer does it belong to consciousness; it is not an activating thought process put into practice, nor is it even a duty that would impose itself from without and from within. *My* responsibility for the Other presupposes an overturning such that it can only be marked by a change in the status of "me," a change in time and perhaps in language. Responsibility, which withdraws me from my order—perhaps from all orders and from order itself—responsibility, which separates me from myself (from the "me" that is mastery and power, from the free, speaking subject) and reveals the other *in place* of me, requires that I answer for absence, for passivity. It requires, that is to say, that I answer for the impossibility of being responsible—to which it has always already consigned me by holding me accountable and also discounting me altogether.[9] And this paradox leaves nothing intact—not subjectivity any more than the subject, not the individual any more than the person. For if I can speak of responsibility only by separating it from all forms of present-consciousness (from will, resolution, concern; from light, from reflective action; but perhaps from the involuntary as well: from all

that is indifferent to my consent, from the gratuitous, the nonacti-
vating, and from the obscurity which derives from the relation consciousness-unconsciousness), if responsibility is rooted where there is
no foundation, where no root can lodge itself, and if thus it tears
clean through all bases and cannot be assumed by any individual
being, how then, how otherwise than as response to the impossible,
and through a relation which forbids me to posit myself at all (if not
as always posited in advance, or presupposed, and this delivers me to
the utterly passive), will we sustain the enigma of what is announced
in the term "responsibility," the term which the language of ordinary morality uses in the most facile way possible by putting it into
the service of order? If responsibility is such that it disengages the
me from me, the singular from the individual, the subjective from
the subject, unawareness from consciousness and the unconscious,
the better to expose me to the nameless passivity, and if responsibility achieves this to such a degree that it is through passivity alone
that I can answer to the infinite demand, then I can certainly call the
response responsibility, but only abusively, naming it by its contrary, knowing all along that to acknowledge responsibility for God
is only a metaphorical means of annulling responsibility (the burden
that weighs upon one as the obligation to assume it), just as, once
declared responsible for dying (for all dying), I can no longer appeal
to any ethics, any experience, any practice whatever—save that of
some counter-living, which is to say an un-practice, or (perhaps) a
word of writing.

But then, the word "responsibility"—contrasting as it does with
our reason without thereby consigning us to some facile irrationality—comes as though from an unknown language which we only
speak counter to our heart and to life, and unjustifiably, just as we
are unjustifiable with respect to every death, to the death of the
Other, and to our own, our own ever improper death. One would
have thus to turn toward some language that never has been written—a language never inscribed but that is always to be pre-
scribed—in order that this incomprehensible word be understood in

its disastrous heaviness and in its way of summoning us to turn toward the disaster without either understanding it or bearing it. That is why responsibility is itself disastrous—the responsibility that never lightens the Other's burden (never lightens the burden he is for me), and makes us mute as far as the word we owe him is concerned.

And yet, to the proximity of the most distant, to the pressure of the most weightless, to the contact of what does not reach us—it is in *friendship* that I can respond, a friendship unshared, without reciprocity, friendship for that which has passed leaving no trace. This is passivity's response to the un-presence of the unknown.

◆ Passivity is a task—but in a different language: in the language of the nondialectical drive—just as negativity is a task in the language wherein the dialectic proposes to us the realization of all possibilities, provided we know how (by cooperating with time through power and mastery in the world) to let time take all its time. The necessity of living and dying according to this double task and in the ambiguity of time—time bereft of present *and* time as history, capable of exhausting (so as to accede to the fulfillment of presence) all the possibilities of time—such is the irreparable decision, the inevitable madness, which is not the content of thought, for thought does not contain it, any more than either consciousness or unconsciousness offers it a determining status. Whence the temptation to appeal to ethics, with its conciliating function (justice and responsibility). But when ethics goes mad in its turn, as it must, what does it contribute if not a safe-conduct which allows our conduct no rights, leaves us no space to move and ensures us of no salvation? It allows only the endurance of a double patience, for patience is double too—speakable, unspeakable patience.

◆ The use of the word "subjectivity" is as enigmatic as the use of the word "responsibility"—and more debatable. For it is a designation chosen, in a way, to preserve our portion of spirituality. Why subjectivity, if not in order to descend clear to the bottom of the

subject without ever losing the prerogative which the subject em-
bodies, that private presence which the body, my sensate body
causes me to live as mine? But if so-called subjectivity is the other *in*
place of me, it is no more subjective than objective; the other is without interiority. Anonymity is the name, and outside is the thought
of the other; his hold on me is that of irrelevance and his time that of
sheer return, just as the neutrality and passivity of dying would be
his life, if it is true that the life of the other is that which must be
welcomed by the gift of the ultimate, the gift of that which (in the
body and through the body) is not — mine — to give.

♦ Passivity is not simple receptivity, any more than it is formless
and inert matter *ready* for any form. Passive are the throes of dying
(dying, silent intensity; that which cannot be welcomed, which is
inscribed wordlessly; the body in the past, the body of no one, of the
interval: being's suspense, a seizure like a cut in time, which we cannot evoke except as wild, unnarratable history having no meaning in
any present). Passive: the un-story, that which escapes quotation
and which memory does not recall — forgetfulness as thought. That
which, in other words, cannot be forgotten because it has always
already fallen outside memory.

♦ I call disaster that which does not have the ultimate for a limit: it
bears the ultimate away in the disaster.

♦ The disaster does not put me into question, but annuls the question, makes it disappear — as if along with the question, "I" too disappeared in the disaster which never appears. The fact of disappearing is, precisely, not a fact, not an event; it does not happen, not
only because there is no "I" to undergo the experience, but because
(and this is exactly what presupposition means), since the disaster always takes place after having taken place, there cannot possibly be
any experience of it.

♦ When the other is related to me in such a way that the utter
stranger in me answers him in my stead, this answer is the immemo-

rial friendship which cannot be chosen, nor can it be lived in the present. It is an offering; it offers a share of the passivity which has no subject. It is dying, dying outside of the self—the body which belongs to no one, in nonnarcissistic suffering, and joy.

♦ Friendship is not a gift, or a promise; it is not a form of generosity. Rather, this incommensurable relation of one to the other is the outside drawing near in its separateness and inaccessibility. Desire, pure impure desire, is the call to bridge the distance, to die in common through separation. Death suddenly powerless, if friendship is the response that one can hear and make heard only by dying ceaselessly.

♦ Keep silence. Silence cannot be kept; it is indifferent with respect to the work of art which would claim to respect it—it demands a wait which has nothing to await, a language which, presupposing itself as the totality of discourse, would spend itself all at once, disjoin and fragment endlessly.

♦ How can one enter a relation with the passive past, a relation which would itself be incapable of presenting itself in the light of a consciousness (or of absenting itself in the obscurity of any unconsciousness)?

♦ The renunciation of the first-person subject is not a voluntary renunciation, nor, thus, is it an involuntary abdication. When the subject becomes absence, then the absence of a subject, or dying as subject, subverts the whole sequence of existence, causes time to take leave of its order, opens life to its passivity, exposing it to the unknown, to the stranger—to the friendship that never is declared.

♦ Weakness can only be human, even though it be in man the inhuman part, the gravity of un-power, the insouciant levity of the friendship that does not weigh, does not ponder—pensive thoughtlessness, that reserve of thought which cannot be thought.
Passivity neither consents nor refuses: neither yes nor no, without preference, it alone suits the limitlessness of the neutral, the unmas-

tered patience which endures time without resisting. The passive condition is no condition: it is an unconditional which no protection shelters, which no destruction touches, which is as remote from submission as it is bereft of initiative; with it, nothing begins. When we hear the word that has always been uttered already, the (mute) language of beginning over again, then we approach the night which is without darkness. It is the irreducible—the incompatible, that which is not compatible with humanity (the human *species*). Human weakness, which even affliction does not divulge, penetrates us on account of our belonging at every instant to the immemorial past of our death—on account of our being indestructible because always and infinitely destroyed. The infiniteness of our destruction, this is the measure of passivity.

♦ Levinas speaks of the subjectivity of the subject. If one wishes to use this word—why? but why not?—one ought perhaps to speak of a *subjectivity without any subject*: the wounded space, the hurt of the dying, the already dead body which no one could ever own, or ever say of it, *I, my body*. This is the body animated solely by mortal desire: the desire of dying—desire that dies and does not thereby subside.

Solitude or noninteriority, exposure to the outside, boundless dispersion, the impossibility of holding firm, within bounds, enclosed—such is man deprived of humanity, the supplement that supplies nothing.

♦ To answer: there is the answer to the question, but then too, the answer that makes the question possible; and also the one that redoubles the question, makes it last and does not appease it, but on the contrary confers upon it a new brilliance, ensures its sharpness—there is the interrogative answer. Finally, as distant as the absolute, there would be the answer without any inquiry, which no question suits, an answer we know not what to do with, for only friendship, which gives it, can receive it.

The enigma (the secret) is precisely the *absence* of any question—

where there is no room even to introduce a question—without, however, this absence's providing the answer. (Cryptic language.)

♦ *The patience of the concept:* renounce, to begin with, the beginning; know that knowledge is never young, but always ageless, aged in a way that is not the way of old age. Then know that one must not finish too swiftly, that the end is always premature, that it is the haste of the Finite to which one longs to entrust oneself once and for all without foreseeing that the Finite is only the ebb of the Infinite.

♦ Not to answer is the rule—or not to receive any answer. This does not suffice to stop questions. But when the answer is the absence of any answer, then the question in turn becomes the absence of any question (the mortified question). Words pass, return to a past which has never spoken, the past of all speech. It is thus that the disaster, although named, does not figure in language.

♦ *Bonaventura:* "Many times over I was driven from churches because I laughed there, and from brothels because there I wanted to pray." The suicide: "I leave nothing behind me, and it is defiantly that I set out to meet you, God—or Nothingness." "Life is but the belled cap worn by Nothingness. . . . All is Nothingness. . . . By this halt of Time, fools mean Eternity, but in truth it is perfect Nothingness, and absolute death, for on the contrary life is born only from an uninterrupted death (if one were to take these ideas seriously, they would lead promptly to the madhouse, but, as for myself, I take them only for foolishness . . .)."
    Fichte: "In nature, all death is at the same time birth and it is precisely in death that life reaches its apogee." And Novalis: "A liaison with death is a wedding which grants us a companion for the night." But Bonaventura never thinks of death as a link to any hope of transcendence: "God be praised! There is a death, and afterwards, there is no Eternity."

♦ Patience is extreme urgency: I no longer have time, says patience (or the time that is left patience is the absence of time, the time before the beginning—the time of un-appearance when one dies un-phenomenally, unbeknownst to all and to oneself, wordlessly, without leaving any trace and thus without dying: patiently).

♦ *Bonaventura:* "I saw myself alone with myself in Nothingness.
. . . Along with Time, all diversity had disappeared, and there reigned only an immense and terrifying lassitude, forever vacant. Beside myself, separated, I tried to annihilate myself, but I remained, and felt myself to be immortal."

♦ Novalis's affirmation, often misquoted or hastily translated: the true philosophical act is the putting to death of oneself (the dying of the self, or the self as dying—*Selbsttötung*, not *Selbstmord*—the mortal movement of the self—the same—toward the other). Suicide, as this mortal movement of identity, can never be undertaken as a plan or project, because the event of suicide is accomplished within a circle separate from all projects, separate perhaps from all thought or truth, and thus it is felt to be unverifiable, indeed unknowable. Any reason one gives for it, however justifiable, seems unsuitable. To kill oneself is to install oneself in the space forbidden to all, which is to say, forbidden to oneself. *Clandestinity,* the unphenomenal part of the human relation, is the essence of "suicide," which is always hidden, less because death is at issue than because dying—passivity itself—becomes action there and shows itself in the act of disappearing, outside the realm of phenomena. Whoever is tempted by suicide is tempted by the invisible, the faceless secret.

There are reasons to kill oneself, and the act of suicide is not unreasonable, but it encloses him who believes he can accomplish it in a space definitively removed from reason (as well as from its opposite, the irrational)—a space foreign to the will and perhaps to *desire*—so that he who kills himself, even if he seeks to do so spectacularly, departs from the domain of manifest occurrences and enters a zone of "malign opacity" (as Baudelaire says) where, all relations to himself as well as to the other having been broken, there reigns the irrelation, the paradoxical difference, definitive and solemn. This happens before any autonomous decision, without any necessity, and as if by chance, and yet under a pressure such that there is nothing in itself passive enough to resist (or even to undergo) its attraction.

◆ Of thought, it must first of all be said that it is the impossibility of sticking to anything definite—the impossibility, then, of thinking of anything determined—and that it is thus the permanent neutralization of all present thought at the same time that it is the repudiation of all absence of thought. Oscillation (paradoxical equality) is the risk run by thought which is abandoned to this double requirement and which does not know that it must be sovereignly patient—in other words, passive outside of all sovereignty.

◆ *Patience, belated perseverence.*

◆ I would speak not of thought that is passive, but would evoke rather a passive that is thought—an always already past of thought—that which, in thought, cannot make itself present, or enter into presence, and is still less able to be represented or to constitute itself as a basis for a representation. Of this passive, nothing else can be said except that it forbids all presence of thought—all power to conduct thought as far as presence (as far as being). This is not to say, though, that it confines thought to a preserve, a retreat outside of presence. Rather, it leaves thought be—close: with the closeness of distance, the closeness of the other, the thought of the other, the other as thought.

◆ *When all is said, what remains to be said is the disaster. Ruin of words, demise writing, faintness faintly murmuring: what remains without remains* (the fragmentary).

◆ The passive need not take place. Rather, implicated in the turn which deviates from the ever-turning, circuitous path and becomes in this way—with respect to the longest tour—a detour, the passive is the torment of the time which has always already passed and which comes thus as a return without any present. It comes without arriving in the patience of the unrecountable era. This is the era destined to the intermittence of a language unburdened of words and dispossessed, the silent halt of that to which without obligation one must nonetheless answer. And such is the responsibility of writing—writing which distinguishes itself by deleting from itself all distinguishing marks, which is to say perhaps, ultimately, by effacing itself (right away *and* at length: this takes all of time), for it seems to leave indelible or indiscernible traces.

◆ *Fragment: beyond fracturing, or bursting, the patience of pure impatience, the little by little suddenly.*

◆ The other is related only to the other: the other repeats, but this repetition is not a repetition of the same; the other redoubles by dividing and diverging infinitely from himself, affirming a time outside of any future, present, or past (a time which the other thus negates)—a time that has always already run out. The Other cannot consent to affirm himself as the Utterly Other, for alterity does not let him rest but works upon him unproductively, displacing him ever so slightly, completely, immeasurably, so that escaping the recognition of the law and of every denomination whatsoever, the other—desire without either a desiring subject or desired object—marks the secret (the separation) of dying: the dying which is in play in every living being and which removes each (ceaselessly, little by little, and every time all at once) from itself as identity, as unity, and as vital becoming.

◆ What Plato teaches us about Plato in the myth of the cave is that men in general are deprived of the power or the right to turn, or to turn back.

◆ To converse, it seems, is not only to turn away from saying what, thanks to language, *is*—the present of a presence. To converse is also to turn language away from itself, maintaining it outside of all unity, outside even the unity of that which is. To converse is to divert language from itself by letting it differ and defer, answering with an always already to a never yet.

◆ In Plato's cave, there is no word to designate death, and no dream or image to intimate its unspeakableness. Death is there, in the cave, as excess, and forgetfully; it arrives from outside into the words of the philosopher as that which reduces him in advance to silence; or, it enters him the better to set him adrift in the futility of a semblance of immortality, making of him a mere shade, the perpetuation of shadow. Death is named solely as the necessity to kill those who, having freed themselves—having had access to the light—come back and reveal, thereby troubling order, disturbing the tranquility of the shelter, and thus desheltering. Death is the act of killing. And the philosopher is he who undergoes the supreme violence. But he also calls upon it, for the truth which he bears and which he tells by his return is a form of violence.

◆ Ironical death: Socrates's, perhaps—the death which death takes away with it and renders thus as discrete as unreal. And if the "possibility" of writing is linked to the "possibility" of irony, then we understand why the one and the other are always disappointing: it is impossible to lay claim to either; both exclude all mastery (cf. Sylviane Agacinski).

◆ We cannot recall our dreams, they cannot come back to us. If a dream comes—but what sort of coming is a dream's? Through what night does it make its way? If it comes to us, it does so only by way of forgetfulness, a forgetfulness which is not only censorship or simply repression. We dream without memory, in such a way that the dream of any particular night is no doubt a fragment of a response to an immemorial dying, barred by desire's repetitiousness.

There is no stop, there is no interval between dreaming and waking. In this sense, it is possible to say: never, dreamer, can you awake (nor, for that matter, are you able to be addressed thus, summoned).

♦ *The dream is without end, waking is without beginning; neither one nor the other ever reaches itself. Only dialectical language relates them to each other in view of a truth.*

♦ Thinking otherwise than he thinks, he thinks in such a way that the Other might come to thought, as approach and response.

♦ *The writer, his biography: he died; lived and died.*

♦ If the book could for a first time really begin, it would, for one last time, long since have ended.

♦ What causes us to fear and desire the new is that the new combats the (established) truth. This is among the most ancient of battles through which right can always be advanced.

♦ *Before it is there, no one awaits it; when it is there, no one recognizes it: for it is not there—the disaster. It has already diverted the word "be," realizing itself to such a degree that it has not begun. A rose blossoming into a bud.*

♦ *When all is obscured, there reigns the clarity without light which certain utterances foretell.*

♦ In praise of life without which it would not be given us to live in accordance with the movement of dying.

♦ The disaster is such that while triumph, glory are not its opposites, neither are they by any means part of it, despite the common wisdom which in the summit already foresees the decline; it has no contrary, and it is not the Simple (whence the fact that nothing is more foreign to it than the dialectic, even if the dialectic were reduced to its destructive moment).

♦ *He questions us: what we do, how we live, who are our friends. He is discreet, as if his questions did not question. And when in our turn we ask him what he does, he smiles, rises, and it is as if he had never been present. Things run their course. He does not trouble us.*

◆ The inexperience of dying. This also means: awkwardness in dying, dying as someone would who has not learned how, or who has missed his classes.

◆ The new, because it cannot take its place in history, is also that which is most ancient: an unhistorical occurrence to which we are called upon to answer as if it were the impossible, the invisible — that which has always long since disappeared beneath ruins.

◆ How could we know that we are forerunners, if the message which ought to make of us messengers is ahead of us by an eternity, condemning us to be eternally tardy?

We are precursors, running along outside of ourselves, out in front of ourselves; when we arrive, our time is past already, and the course of things interrupted.

◆ If quotations, in their fragmenting force, destroy in advance the texts from which they are not only severed but which they exalt till these texts become nothing but severence, then the fragment without a text, or any context, is radically unquotable.

◆ *Why did all afflictions — finite, infinite, personal, impersonal, current, timeless — imply and ceaselessly recall the historically dated affliction, which is nevertheless without any date, of a country already so reduced that it seemed almost effaced from the map and whose history nonetheless exceeded the history of the world? Why?*

◆ *He writes — does he write? — not because the books of others leave him unsatisfied (on the contrary, they all please him), but because they are books and because by writing one does not get enough.*

◆ Write in order that the negative and the neutral, in their always concealed difference — in the most dangerous of proximities — might recall to each other their respective specificity, the one working, the other un-working. [10]

◆ Today is poor; this poverty — which would be essential to today if

it were not extreme to the point of possessing no essence—permits
today not to accede to presence, and not to delay in the new or in the
old of any now.

♦ Write in order not simply to destroy, in order not simply to con-
serve, in order not to transmit; write in the thrall of the impossible
real, that share of disaster wherein every reality, safe and sound,
sinks.

♦ Trust in language is the opposite—distrust of language—situated within language. Confidence in language is language itself dis-
trusting—defying—language: finding in its own space the unshak-
able principles of a critique. Whence the recourse to etymology (or
the refusal to acknowledge any value in it); whence the appeal to
anagrammatical entertainments, to acrobatic inversions whose in-
tent is to multiply words infinitely on the pretext of deforming
them, but in vain. All this is justified on the condition that it all (recourse and refusal) be employed at once, at the same time, without
belief in any of it, and without cease. The unknown of language remains unknown—the stranger foreign.

Trust-distrust in language is already fetishism; it amounts to
choosing a particular word in order to play on it with the delight
and the malaise of the perversion that always assumes a straight, if
hidden, usage. But writing: the detour that would disqualify the
right to any language at all (even to a twisted, anagrammatized one)
—the detour of inscription (which is always a de-scription). . . .
Writing, friendship for the ill-come unknown, for the "reality" that
cannot be made evident and that escapes every possible utterance.

A writer in spite of himself: it is not a matter of writing despite or
against oneself in a relation of contradiction—indeed, of incompati-
bility—with oneself, or with life, or with writing (that is all merely
the biography of the writer, and he has only anecdotal significance).
Rather, it is a matter of writing in another relation, from which the
other dismisses himself and has always dismissed us, even in the
movement of attraction. Whence the vain names—reality, glory, or

disaster—whereby that which separates itself from language consecrates itself therein—or whereby it falls into language, from loss of
patience, perhaps. For it could be that all names—and precisely the
last, unpronounceable one—are an effect of impatience.

♦ Light breaks forth: the burst of light, the dispersion that reso-
nates or vibrates dazzlingly—and in clarity clamors but does not
clarify. The breaking forth of light, the shattering reverberation of a
language to which no hearing can be given.

♦ Dying to no end: thus (through this movement of immobility)
would thought fall outside all teleology and perhaps outside its site.
To think endlessly, the way one dies—this is the thinking that
patience in its innocent perseverence seems to impose. And this endlessness implies not gratuity but responsibility. Whence the repeated, motionless step of the speechless unknown, there at our
door, on the threshold.
    To think the way one dies: without purpose, without power,
without unity, and precisely, without "the way." Whence the
effacement of this formulation as soon as it is thought—as soon as it
is thought, that is, both on the side of thinking and of dying, in dis-
equilibrium, in an excess of meaning and in excess of meaning. No
sooner is it thought than it has departed; it is gone, outside.
    Thinking as dying excludes the "as" of thought, in a manner such
that even if we suppress this "as" by paratactic simplification and
write "to think: to die," it forms an enigma in its absence, a practically unbridgeable space. The un-relation of thinking and dying is
also the form of their relation: not that thinking proceeds toward
dying, proceeding thus toward its other, but not that it proceeds toward its likeness either. It is thus that "as" acquires the impetuous-
ness of its meaning: neither like nor different, neither other nor
same.
    Between thinking and dying there is a sort of downward ascen-
dance: the more we think in the absence of any (determined)

thought, the more we rise, step by step, toward the precipice, the sheer fall, headlong. To think is naught but ascent or decline, but it has no determined thought to stop at and so return toward itself. Whence its vertigo, which is, however, equilibrium—its precipitousness, which is, nonetheless, level and even—just as to die is always even, equal (lethal).

◆ If spirit is always active, then patience is already nonspirit: the body in its suffering passivity—cadaverous, exposed, flattened, sheer surface. Patience is the cry beneath the word: not the spirit; the letter. And in this sense life itself, as the shade of life, the gift or living expenditure even unto dying.

◆ "Already" or "always already" marks the disaster, which is outside history, but historically so: before undergoing it, we (who is not included in this we?) will undergo it. It is a trance, motionless transgression, the passiveness of the passage beyond. The disaster is the improperness of its name and the disappearance of the proper name (Derrida); it is neither noun nor verb, but a remainder which would bar with invisibility and illegibility all that shows and is said—a remainder which is neither a result (as in subtraction), nor a quantity left over (as in division). Patience again—the passive. The *Aufhebung* turns inoperable, ceases. Hegel: "Innocence alone is nonaction (the absence of operation)."

◆ The disaster is the time when one can no longer—by desire, ruse, or violence—risk the life which one seeks, through this risk, to prolong. It is the time when the negative falls silent and when in place of men comes the infinite calm (the effervescence) which does not embody itself or make itself intelligible.

◆ *They do not think of death, having no other relation but with death.*

◆ A reading of what once was written: *he who masters death (finite life) unleashes the infinitude of dying.*

◆ The passivity of language: if one employs Hegelian language (falsifying it somewhat) one can affirm that the concept is death, the end of natural and of spiritual life, but that dying is the dark side of life, the far side with no action, the beyond without being—life without death. The perishable itself, in other words. The eternally perishable, which penetrates us while interminably we finish speaking, speaking as though after the finish, listening without speaking to the echo of that which has always already passed and which comes to pass nonetheless: the passage.

◆ *The other is always someone else, and this someone is always other than himself; he is relieved of all propriety, all proper sense, and thus beyond every mark of truth and sign of light.*

◆ Dying is, speaking absolutely, the incessant imminence whereby life lasts, desiring. The imminence of what has always already come to pass.

◆ Suffering suffers from being innocent: thus it seeks to become guilty in order to lessen. But the passivity in it eludes delinquency: perfectly passive is suffering, safe from the thought of salvation.

◆ There is disaster only because, ceaselessly, it falls short of disaster. The end of nature, the end of culture.

◆ *The danger that the disaster acquire meaning instead of body.*

◆ To write, "to form," where no forms hold sway, an absent meaning. Absent meaning (and not the absence of meaning or a potential or latent but lacking sense). To write is perhaps to bring to the surface something like absent meaning, to welcome the passive pressure which is not yet what we call thought, for it is already the disastrous ruin of thought. Thought's patience. Between the disaster and the other there would be the contact, the disjunction of absent meaning—friendship. An absent meaning would maintain "the affirmation" of a push pushing beyond loss, the pressure of dying that bears loss off with it. Lost loss. This meaning does not pass by way of being, it never reaches so far; it is expired meaning. Whence the difficulty of a commentary on writing: for commentary signifies and produces signification, unable as it is to sustain an absent meaning.

♦ Desire of writing, writing of desire. Desire of knowledge, knowledge of desire. Let us not believe that we have said anything at all with these reversals. Desire, writing, do not remain in place, but pass one over the other: these are not plays on words, for desire is always the desire of dying, not a wish. And yet, desire is related to *Wunsch,* and is a nondesire too — the powerless power that traverses writing — just as writing is the desired, undesired torment which endures everything, even impatience. Dying desire, desire to die, we live these together — not that they coincide — in the obscurity of the interim.

♦ *Keep watch over absent meaning.*

♦ It is confirmed, in and by incertitude, that not every fragment is related to the fragmentary. The fragmentary — the "power" of the disaster which none has experienced, and the disastrous intensity, incommensurate with pleasure, with joy — is marked; that is, its every distinguishing mark is deleted, and the fragment would be this mark, always threatened by some success or other. There cannot be a successful, a satisfactory fragment, or one indicating the end at last, the cessation of error, and this would be the case if for no other reason than that every fragment, though unique, repeats, and is undone by repetition.

Let us remember. Repetition: nonreligious repetition, neither mournful nor nostalgic, the undesired return. Repetition: the ultimate over and over, general collapse, destruction of the present.

♦ Knowledge becomes finer and lighter only at the outer edges, when truth no longer constitutes the principle to which it must finally submit. The nontrue, which is not falsehood, draws knowledge outside of the system, into the space of an aimless drifting where key words no longer dominate, where repetition does not serve meaning (but is the ultimate collapse, of the ultimate) —

where knowledge, without passing into un-knowledge, no longer depends upon itself, and neither results nor produces a result, but changes imperceptibly, effacing itself: no longer knowledge, but a likeness thereof.

In the knowledge which must always free itself from knowledge, there is none prior; nor does this knowledge succeed itself, and there is thus no presence of knowledge either. Do not apply a knowledge; do not repeat it. Enough of theory which wields and organizes knowledge. Here space opens to "fictive theory," and theory, through fiction, comes into danger of dying. You theoreticians, know that you are mortal, and that theory is already death in you. Know this, be acquainted with your companion. Perhaps it is true that "without theorizing, you would not take one step forward," but this step is one more step toward the abyss of truth. Thence rises the silent murmuring, the tacit intensity.

When the domination of truth ceases — that is, when the reference to the true-false dichotomy (and to the union of the two) no longer holds sway, not even as the task of a language yet to come — then knowledge continues to seek itself and to seek to inscribe itself, but in an other space where there is no longer any direction. When knowledge is no longer a knowledge of truth, it is then that knowledge starts: a knowledge that burns thought, like knowledge of infinite patience.

◆ When Kafka allows a friend to understand that he writes because otherwise he would go mad, he knows that writing is madness already, his madness, a kind of vigilence, unrelated to any wakefulness save sleep's: insomnia. Madness against madness, then. But he believes that he masters the one by abandoning himself to it; the other frightens him, and is his fear; it tears through him, wounds and exalts him. It is as if he had to undergo all the force of an uninterruptable continuity, a tension at the edge of the insupportable which he speaks of with fear and not without a feeling of glory. For glory is the disaster.

◆ Accept this distinction: "it is necessary" and not "you must"—
perhaps because the second formula is addressed to a *you* and the first
is an affirmation outside law, without legality, an unnecessary necessity. All the same, an affirmation? a manifestation of violence? I
seek a passive "it is necessary," worn out by patience.

◆ *But something binds me to this ancient adventure, infinite and foreign to
meaning, though all the while, at the heart of the disaster, I continue to seek
it as that which does not come, and to await it, when it is the patience of my
waiting.*

◆ Let us suppose that everyone has his private madness. Knowledge
without truth would be the labor or the attention of an intense singularity analogous to this "private" madness—for everything private is madness to the extent at least that we seek, through it, to
communicate.

◆ If the dilemma is to go mad or to die, then the answer will not
lack and madness will be mortal.

◆ *In his dream, nothing, nothing but the desire to dream.*

◆ When I say, following Nietzsche, *"il faut"* ["it is necessary"]—
with the play between *falloir* [be necessary] and *faillir* [fail]—I also
say, it lacks, falls short, deceives. Such is the beginning of the
downfall: in its very failing the law commands, and thereby escapes
safe and sound yet again as law.

◆ He is able to read (a book, a piece of writing, a text—not always,
not always, and is he able to?) because he preserves, losing it, a certain relation with to write. This does not mean that he reads more
gladly what makes him want to write—to write without desire belongs to patience, the passivity of writing—but rather that he reads
more willingly what inflames writing, makes its violence flare up by
destroying it or, more simply, more mysteriously, what is in a relation with the immemorial passive, with anonymity, absolute discretion, human weakness.

♦ Never an attempt to make writing untamable — writing, exposed to all the winds of reductive commentary, always already caught and detained, or spurned.

♦ The law's scheme: that prisoners construct their prison themselves. This is the culmination of the concept, and the concept is the mark of the system.

♦ In the Hegelian system (that is, in all systems), death is constantly in operation, and nothing dies, nothing can die. What remains after the system — the naught left over, still to be expended — is the push of dying in its repetitive novelty.

♦ The word "body," its danger, how easily it gives one the illusory impression of being outside of meaning already, free from the contamination of consciousness-unconsciousness. Insidious return of the natural, of Nature. The body does not belong; it is mortal immortal; it is unreal, imaginary, fragmentary. Patient. In its patientness the body is thought already — still just thought.

♦ To say, I like Sade, is to have no relation at all to Sade. Sade cannot be liked, no one can stand him, for what he writes turns us away absolutely by attracting us absolutely: the attraction of the detour.

We have destroyed him, we have freed the star — henceforth without radiance: dark he wheels, the star of disaster, vanished as he wished it, in the anonymous tomb of his renown.

But it is quite true that there is irony in Sade (there is in his writing the power that is dissolution's): whoever does not sense it reads a commonplace writer with a system. There is nothing in Sade that can be called serious; or rather, his seriousness is the mockery of seriousness, just as *passion passes* through Sade in a moment of coolness, of secretness, of neutrality. Apathy, the infinite passivity. This is the grand irony — not Socratic, not feigned ignorance — but saturation by impropriety (when nothing whatsoever suits anymore), the grand dissimulation where all is said, all is said again and finally silenced.

♦ Never either-or, simple logic. And never two at once, the two
that always end up affirming each other dialectically or compulsively
(antagonism without any risk to it). All dualism, all binaries draw
thought into the conveniences of exchanges: the accounts will all be
settled. Eros Thanatos: two forces yet again; but duality does not
rule; the One does. Division does not suffice, this dialectic is realized. There is not *the* death drive; the throes of death are thefts from
unity, lost multitudes.

♦ I return to the fragment: while it never is unique, still it has no
external limit—the outside toward which it falls is not its edge—
and at the same time no internal limitation (it is no hedgehog,
rolled up and closed upon itself). And yet it is something strict, not
because of its brevity (it can be prolonged like agony), but through
the tautness, the tightness that chokes to the breaking point: there
are always some links that have sprung (they are not missing). No
fullness, no void.

♦ Writing is per se already (it is still) violence: the rupture there is
in each fragment, the break, the splitting, the tearing of the
shred—acute singularity, steely point. And yet this combat is, for
patience, debate. The name wears away, the fragment fragments,
erodes. Passivity passes away patiently, lost stakes.

♦ To be lost, to capsize. Desire of the fall, desire which is the push
and the pull of the fall. And whoever falls is not one, but several.
Multiple fall. Each one restrains himself, clinging to an other, an
other who is himself and is the dissolution—the dispersion—of the
self, and the restraint is sheer haste, panicky flight, death outside
death.

♦ One cannot "read" Hegel, except by not reading him. To read,
not to read him—to understand, to misunderstand him, to reject
him—all this falls under the authority of Hegel or doesn't take
place at all. Only the intensity of this nonoccurrence, in the impossibility that there be such a thing, prepares us for a death—the

death of reading, the death of writing—which leaves Hegel living: the living travesty of completed Meaning. (Hegel the impostor: this is what makes him invincible, mad with his seriousness, counterfeiter of Truth: "putting one over" to the point of becoming, all unbeknownst to him, master of irony—Sylviane Agacinski.)

◆ What is it that rings false in the system? What makes it limp? The question itself is immediately unsteady and does not amount to a question. What exceeds the system is the impossibility of its failure, and likewise the impossibility of its success. Ultimately nothing can be said of it, and there is a way of keeping still (the lacunary silence of writing), that halts the system, leaving it idle, delivered to the seriousness of irony.

◆ Knowledge at rest. Unsuitable terms, but no matter: we can only let fragmentary writing write if language, having exhausted its power of negation, its force of affirmation, retains or sustains Knowledge at rest. This is writing that is outside language: it is nothing else, perhaps, but the end (without end) of knowledge, the end of myths, the erosion of utopia, the rigor of taut patience.

◆ *The unknown name, alien to naming:*
   The holocaust, the absolute *event of history—which is a date in history—that utter-burn where all history took fire, where the movement of Meaning was swallowed up, where the gift, which knows nothing of forgiving or of consent, shattered without* giving *place to anything that can be affirmed, that can be denied—gift of very passivity, gift of what cannot be given. How can it be preserved, even by thought? How can thought be made the keeper of the holocaust where all was lost, including guardian thought?*
   In the mortal intensity, the fleeing silence of the countless cry.

◆ There is in death, it would seem, something stronger than death: it is dying itself—the intensity of dying, the push of the impossible, the pressure of the undesirable even in the most desired. Death is power and even strength—limited, therefore. It sets a final date, it adjourns in the sense that it assigns to a given day [*jour*]— both random and necessary—at the same time that is defers till an undesignated day. But dying is un-power. It wrests from the present, it is always a step over the edge, it rules out every conclusion and all ends, it does not free nor does it shelter. In death, one can find an illusory refuge: the grave is as far as gravity can pull, it marks the end of the fall; the mortuary is the loophole in the impasse. But dying flees and pulls indefinitely, impossibly and intensively in the flight.

◆ The *disappointment* of the disaster: not answering to expectations, not allowing the point to be made or the appointed sum paid in full—foreign to orientation, even to orientation as disorientation or simple straying.

◆ Desire remains in a relation to the distantness of the star, entreating the sky, appealing to the universe. In this sense, the disaster would turn us away from desire with the intense attraction of the undesirable impossible.

◆ Lucidity, ray of the star, response to the day that questions, and sleep when night comes. "But who will hide from the star that never sets?" Wakefulness is without beginning or end. To wake is neutral. "I" do not wake: someone does, the night does, always and incessantly, hollowing the night out into the other night where there can be no question of sleeping. There is no waking save at night. Night is foreign to the vigilance which is exercised, carried out, and which conveys lucid reason toward what it must maintain in reflection—in the preservation, that is, of its own identity. Wakefulness is estrangement: it does not waken, as if emerging from a sleep that would precede it, yet it reawakens: constant and instant return to the immobility of the wake. Something wakes: something keeps watch without lying in wait or spying. The disaster watches. When there is such watching—when sleeping consciousness, opening into unconsciousness, lets the light of the dream play—then what watches (the wake, or the impossibility of sleep at the heart of sleep) does not illuminate with an increase of visibility, of reflecting brilliance. Who watches? The question is obviated by the neutrality of the watch: no one watches. Watching is not the power to keep watch — in the first person; it is not a power, but the touch of the powerless infinite, exposure to the other of the night, where thought renounces the vigor of vigilance, gives up worldly clearsightedness, perspicacious mastery, in order to deliver itself to the limitless deferral of insomnia, the wake that does not waken, nocturnal intensity.

♦ It might be said that within the disaster there occurs a falling short, if it were not also characteristic of the disaster to be a trance: the motionless fall and flight of the outside. Deficiency does not let the exception rest on high, but causes a ceaseless fall (without form or content), outside the attainable and the possible. The exceptional escapes, deficiency dissimulates. Consciousness can be catastrophic without ceasing to be consciousness; it does not reverse itself, turning into its opposite, but welcomes into itself this overturning. Only such re-turning, that wrests from the present, detours consciousness-unconsciousness.[11]

♦ In the night, insomnia is dis-cussion: not the work of arguments bumping against other arguments, but the extreme shuddering of no thoughts, percussive stillness (the exegeses that come and go in *The Castle,* story of insomnia).

♦ To give is not to give something, or even oneself, for then — inasmuch as what one gives has as its characteristic feature that no one can take it from you (retrieve it from you and withhold it) — to give would be to keep and to preserve. Summit of egotism, ruse of possession. Since the gift is not the power of any freedom, or the sublime act of a free subject, there would be no gift at all if not the gift of what one does not have, under duress and beyond duress, in answer to the entreaty which strips and flays me and destroys my ability to answer, outside the world, where there is nothing save the attraction and the pressure of the other.[12] Gift of the disaster, of that which can neither be asked for nor given. Gift of the gift, with neither giver nor receiver, which does not annul the gift but which causes nothing to happen in this world of presence and under the sky of absence where things happen, or even do not happen. That is why to speak of loss, of pure loss and in pure loss, seems, even though speech is never secure, still too facile.

♦ Joy, sorrow — try to retain only their intensity, the very low or (it matters not) the very high intensity which is without intention. Then you live neither within nor without yourself, nor close to things, but the quick of life passes and makes you pass *outside sidereal space,* into the presentless time where it is in vain that you would seek yourself.

♦ Desire, still a relation to the star — the great sidereal desire, religious and nostalgic, panicky or cosmic. It is thus that there can be no desire of the disaster. To wake, to watch is not to desire to do so; it is without any such desire, but is the undesirable nocturnal intensity (more, and less than can be desired).

We are not called outside of ourselves by care's obsession, but detained within the region that's secure, even as we make our way to abandon.

The disaster: sign of its approach without approximation. Cares depart to give place to solicitude. *Die sorglose Nacht,* the careless night, when that which cannot awaken keeps watch. But the night, the first night, still keeps busy. This is the night that does not break with the day, and even if, exposed to sleep, one does not sleep, one remains nonetheless in a relation to being-in-the-world; one keeps to the position of the repose which one just happens, on this night, not to find.

If I say: the disaster keeps watch, it is not in order to give a subject to the vigil; it is to say: the wake does not occur under the sidereal sky.

♦ An experience that is not a lived event, and that does not engage the present of presence, is already nonexperience (although negation does not deprive it of the peril of that which comes to pass already past). It is just an excess of experience, and affirmative though it be, in this excess no experience occurs; it cannot posit itself in the instant and find therein repose (mobile though the moment be), or bestow itself lavishly in some point of incandescence: it marks only the exclusion of such a point. We feel that there cannot be any experience of the disaster, even if we were to understand disaster to be the ultimate experience. This is one of its features: it impoverishes all experience, withdraws from experience all authenticity; it keeps its vigil only when night watches without watching over anything.

◆ *May it be a question of Nothing, ever, for Anyone.*

◆ The quick of life would be the burn of a wound—a hurt so lively, a flame so avid that it is not content to live and be present, but consumes all that is present till presence is precisely what is exempt from the present. The quick of life is the exemplarity, in the absence of any example, of un-presence, of un-life; absence in its vivacity always coming back without ever coming.

◆ Silence is perhaps a word, a paradoxical word, the silence of the word *silence*, [13] yet surely we feel that it is linked to the cry, the voiceless cry, which breaks with all utterances, which is addressed to no one and which no one receives, the cry that lapses and decries. Like writing (and in the same way that the quick of life has always already exceeded life), the cry tends to exceed all language, even if it lends itself to recuperation as language effect. It is both sudden and patient; it has the suddenness of the interminable torment which is always over already. [14] The patience of the cry: it does not simply come to a halt, reduced to nonsense, yet it does remain outside of sense—a meaning infinitely suspended, decried, decipherable-indecipherable.

◆ In the work of mourning, it is not grief that works: grief keeps watch.

♦ Grief, incising, dissecting, exposing a hurt which can no longer be endured, or even remembered.

♦ It is not thought that the disaster causes to disappear, but rather questions and problems — affirmation and negation, silence and speech, sign and insignia — from thought. Then, in the night that is without darkness, that has no sky, in the night heavy with the absence of the world and withdrawn from all self-presence, thought watches. What I know, with an inverted, invented, and adjacent knowledge — without any relation of truth — is that such a wake permits neither waking nor sleeping. It leaves thought outside of any secret, deprives it of all intimacy, and turns it into the body of its absence. For it lays thought bare to the lack of thought. And all the while there ceaselessly persists the exchange of lifeless vulnerability and of dying invulnerable to death. The lowest intensity does not make the waiting any shorter; it does not put an end to the infinite deferral. It is as if the wake gently, passively let us descend the perpetual staircase.

♦ A word that is almost deprived of meaning is noisy. Meaning is limited silence (language is relatively silent, depending on the degree to which it contains the element into which it departs, the already departed, the absent meaning, which verges upon the a-semic).

♦ If there is a perseverance principle, an imperative to persist, and if this is the context wherein death is a mystery, then we who are turned away from the star, disturbed in our uncertain certitude of the cosmic order, we who have no longer any situation with respect to the universe and are without the power to consent or acquiesce (we who are in life outside of life) — we have always been delivered by the patience of the utterly passive to the interruption of being: to the pressure of dying which makes us fall under the attraction of the undesirable disaster where continuity in every sense and discontinuity in every sense, given both at once, defeat the seriousness and severity of what perseveres, stubbornly continuing the mortal game.

◆ May what is written resound in the stillness, making silence resound at length, before returning to the motionless peace where the
enigma still wakes.

◆ *Forgo living in the protection of the perseverance principle— being as
perseverance— whence death gets its mystery.*

◆ Writing, without placing itself above art, supposes that one not
prefer art, but efface art as writing effaces itself.

◆ Do not forgive. Forgiveness accuses before it forgives. By accus-
ing, by stating the injury, it makes the wrong irredeemable. It carries the blow all the way to culpability. [15] Thus, all becomes irreparable; giving and forgiving cease to be possible.
   Forgive nothing save innocence.
   Forgive me for forgiving you.
   The sole fault would be one of position: the one and only fault is
to be "I," for it is not identity that the Self in myself brings me.
This self is merely a formal necessity: it simply serves to allow the
infinite relation of Self to Other. Whence the temptation (the sole
temptation) to become a subject again, instead of being exposed to
subjectivity without any subject, the nudity of dying space.
   I cannot forgive— forgiveness comes from others— but I cannot
be forgiven either, if forgiveness is what calls the "I" into question
and demands that I give myself, that I subject myself to the lack of
subjectivity. And if forgiveness comes from others, it only comes;
there is never any certitude that it can arrive, because in it there is
nothing of the (sacramental) power to determine. It can only delay
in the element of indecision. In *The Trial,* one might think that the
death scene constitutes the pardon, the end of the interminable; but
there is no end, since Kafka specifies that shame survives, which is
to say, the infinite itself, a mockery of life as life's beyond.

◆ Inattention: there is inattention which is disdainful insensitivity.
Then there is the more passive inattention which, beyond any interest or calculation, lets others be other, leaving them outside the

sphere of the violence by which they would be caught, grasped, snared, identified, reduced to sameness. This inattention is not the attitude of an I more attentive to self than to others; it distracts me from myself and this distraction strips the "I," exposes it to the passion of the utterly passive, where, with eyes that are open but that look not, I become infinite absence. Then even the affliction that cannot endure to be seen and which vision cannot endure, lets itself be considered, approached, and perhaps calmed. But this inattention remains ambiguous: either scorn so extreme it disdains to appear, or the extreme of discretion, offered to the point of effacement.

♦ What is strange in the Cartesian certitude "I think, therefore I am," is that it only presented itself by speaking, and that speech, precisely, caused it to disappear, suspending the *ego* of the *cogito,* consigning thought to anonymity without any subject — to the intimacy of exteriority — and substituting for living presence (for the existence of the I am) the intense absence of an undesirable and attractive dying. Thus it would suffice that the *ego cogito* be pronounced in order that it cease to be announced and that the indubitable, without falling into doubt, and remaining free of doubtfulness, be, while intact, ruined invisibly by the silence that cleaves language, is the flow of language and, losing itself in language, changes language into its loss. That is why one can say that Descartes never knew he was speaking, any more than that he was keeping still. It is on this condition that the lovely truth is preserved.

♦ For Plato, according to a typically Platonic dialectic — and in a discovery, therefore, which is stunning (and perilous besides, for in some respects it remains to be made) — the other of the other is the Self, the Same. But how can one avoid hearing, in that redoubling, the repetition which reduces to passivity, which voids and disidentifies, withdrawing alterity (the alienating power) from the other without ceasing to let him be other — indeed always more other (an otherness not so much increased as exceeded)—through the consecration of the detour and of the return?

♦ Inattention: the intensity of it. The distantness that keeps watch beyond attention, ensuring that attention not be limited by causing attentiveness merely to something, indeed to someone—indeed to everything. Inattention neither negative nor positive, but excessive, which is to say without intentionality, without reproval, without the displacement that time effects (the ec-stacy); mortal inattention to which we are not free—or able—to consent, or even to let ourselves go (to give ourselves—up); the inattentive, intensely attractive, utterly negligent passion which, while the star shines, marks—under a well-disposed sky and upon the earth that sustains us—the push toward, and the access to the eternal Outside. There the cosmic order still subsists, but as an arrogant, impatient, discredited reign. There, under the inapparent brilliance of sidereal space, in the clearness bereft of light, sovereignty suspended—absent and there, always there—refers endlessly to a dead law which in its very fall, fails yet again, the lawless law of death. The *other* of the law.

♦ *If the break with the star could be accomplished in the manner of an event—if we could (if only through the violence that operates in our bruised space), depart from the cosmic order (the world), where whatever the visible disorder, order always dominates—still, the thought of the disaster, in its adjourned imminence, would lend itself to an experience of discovery whereby we could only be recuperated, not exposed to that which escapes in motionless flight, is separate from the living and from the dying and is not experience, but outside the realm of phenomena.*

♦ Only the rule of moderation can be affirmed or denied. But affirmation, negation have no place when the highest tension, the deepest depression break all relations that could be signified (presented or absented) in an utterance. (The highest tension, the deepest depression: that which vaporizes the always measured rapture—measured even when extremely troubled; that which in suffering has fallen beneath suffering and is too passive still to be suffered; the unendurable calm of suffering.) Then, when all relations that there can be, or else not be, are suspended, affirmation, negation come apart. So undone are they that they reach the neutral which no language can control even though, never ceasing to be displaced from language, it is never separate from language.

Intensity cannot be called high or low without reestablishing the scale of values and principles characteristic of moderation's mediocre morality. Be it exertion or inertia, intensity is the extreme of difference, in excess of the being that ontology takes for granted. Intensity is an excess, an absolute disruption which admits of no regimen, region, regulation, direction, erection, insur-rection, nor does it admit of their simple contraries; thus it wrecks what it makes known, burning the thought which thinks it and yet requiring this thought in the conflagration where transcendence, immanence are no longer anything but flamboyant, extinguished figures—reference points of writing which writing has always lost in advance. For writing excludes the limitless, continuous process just as much as it seems to include a nonmanifest fragmentation—which in its turn, however, presupposes a continuous surface upon which it would be inscribed, just as it presupposes the experience with which it breaks. Thus, writing continues by discontinuity; it is the lure of silence which, in very absence, has already delivered us to the disastrous return.

Intensity: the attractiveness in this name lies not only in its generally escaping conceptualization, but also in its way of coming apart in a plurality of names, de-nominations which dismiss the power that can be exerted as well as the intentionality that orients, and also sign and sense, and the space that unfolds and the time that expatiates. But along with all this comes some confusion, for intensity's name seems to restore a sort of corporeal interiority— vital vibrancy—whereby the faded teachings of consciousness-unconsciousness are imprinted anew. Whence the necessity to say that only exteriority, in its absolute separation, its infinite disintensification, returns to intensity the disastrous attractiveness that keeps it from letting itself be translated into revelation—a surplus of knowledge, of belief—and turns it back into thought, but thought which exceeds itself and is no longer anything but the torment—the tortuousness—of this return.

◆ "Intensity": that different word to which Klossowski has led us in order that it disavow us. He leads us to it by taking care not to make it a key word or a slogan one would have only to invoke in order to open up the gap through which meaning would flow out and fall silent, permitting us thus once and for all to escape its restriction (F. Schlegel: "the infinitude of intensity").

◆ In the silent outside, in the silence of silence which by no means has any relation to language for it does not come from language but has always already departed from it—in this silent exteriority, that which has neither begun nor ever will finish, keeps watch: the night: the night where for the other an other is substituted—the other whom Descartes tried to determine by picturing him as the Great Contradictor, the deceitful Other who has for his role not only to make light of evidence (of the manifestly visible), or to pursue the work of doubt (duplicity, the simple splitting of the One whereby the One continues to preserve itself), but who undermines the other as other. Whereupon the possibility of illusion and of seriousness, of deceit and equivocation, of the mute word and also of speaking muteness collapses. No longer can mockery give any indication at all, not even a meaningless one, even though, conveyed by the silence of silence (by this repetition)—by the silence that does not come from any language (it is, however language's outside)—there emerges this travesty, the disastrous return (death arrested).

◆ These names, areas of dislocation, the four winds of spirit's absence, breath from nowhere—the names of thought, when it lets itself come undone and, by writing, fragment. Outside. Neutral.

Disaster. Return. Surely these names form no system. In their abruptness, like proper names designating no one, they slide outside all possible meaning without this slide's meaning anything—it leaves only a sliding half-gleam that clarifies nothing, not even the outside, whose frontier is nowhere indicated. These names, in a devastated field, ravaged by the absence which has preceeded them—and which they would bear within themselves if it weren't that, empty of all interiority, they rise up exterior to themselves (stones petrified by the endlessness of their fall and forming the walls of an abyss)—seem remainders, each one, of an other language, both disappeared and never yet pronounced, a language we cannot even attempt to restore without reintroducing these names back into the world, or exalting them to some higher world of which, in their external, clandestine solitude, they could only be the irregular interruption, the invisible retreat.

◆ *Always returning upon the paths of time, we are neither ahead nor behind: late is early, near far.*

◆ Fragments are written as unfinished separations. Their incompletion, their insufficiency, the disappointment at work in them, is their aimless drift, the indication that, neither unifiable nor consistent, they accommodate a certain array of marks—the marks with which thought (in decline and declining itself) represents the furtive groupings that fictively open and close the absence of totality. Not that thought ever stops, definitively fascinated, at the absence; always it is carried on, by the watch, the ever-uninterrupted wake. Whence the impossibility of saying there is an interval. For fragments, destined partly to the blank that separates them, find in this gap not what ends them, but what prolongs them, or what makes them await their prolongation—what has already prolonged them, causing them to persist on account of their incompletion. And thus are they always ready to let themselves be worked upon by indefatigable reason, instead of remaining as fallen utterances, left aside, the secret void of mystery which no elaboration could ever fill.

♦ Upon reading this sentence from years ago: "Inspiration, that errant language which cannot end, is the long night of insomnia, and it is to defend against this night—it is by turning away from it—that the writer comes actually to write, an activity which restores him to the world where he can sleep"; or: "Where I am dreaming, something wakes, a vigilance which is the unexpectedness of the dream and where in fact there keeps watch, in a present without duration, a presence without subject, the un-presence to which no being ever accedes and whose grammatical formulation would be a third person. . . . " Why this recollection? Why is it that despite what they say about the uninterrupted wake which persists behind the dream, and about the inspirational night of insomnia, still these words seem to need to be taken up again, repeated, in order to escape the meaning that animates them, and to be turned away from themselves, from the discourse that employs them? But, taken up anew, they reintroduce an assurance to which one thought one had ceased to subscribe. They have an air of truth; they say something— they aspire to coherence. They say: you thought all this long ago; you are thus authorized to think it again. They restore this reasonable continuity which forms systems; they employ the past as a guarantee, letting it become active; it cites, incites. Thus they prevent the invisible ruin which the perpetual wake, outside consciousness-unconsciousness, gives back to the neutral.

♦ The language of awaiting—perhaps it is silent, but it does not separate speaking and silence; it makes of silence already a kind of speaking; already it says in silence the speaking that silence is. For mortal silence does not keep still.

♦ Fragmentary writing is risk, it would seem: risk itself. It is not based on any theory, nor does it introduce a practice one could define as *interruption*. Interrupted, it goes on. Interrogating itself, it does not co-opt the question but suspends it (without maintaining it) as nonresponse. Thus, if it claims that its time comes only when the whole—at least ideally—is realized, this is because that time is never sure, but is the absence of time, absence in a nonnegative sense, time anterior to all past-present, as well as posterior to every possibility of a present yet to come.

♦ If there is, among all words, one that is inauthentic, then surely it is the word "authentic."

♦ The demand, the extreme demand of the fragmentary is at first obeyed lazily, as though it were a matter of stopping at fragments, sketches, studies: preparations or rejected versions of what is not yet a work. That this demand traverses, overturns, ruins the work because the work (totality, perfection, achievement) is the unity which is satisfied with itself— this is what F. Schlegel sensed, but it is also what finally escaped him, though in such a way that one cannot reproach him with this misunderstanding which he helped and still helps us to discern in the very movement whereby we share it with him. The fragmentary imperative, linked to the disaster. That there is, however, practically nothing disastrous in this disaster: this is surely what we must learn to think, without, perhaps, ever knowing it.

♦ Fragmentation, the mark of a coherence all the firmer in that it has to come undone in order to be reached, and reached not through a dispersed system, or through dispersion as a system, for fragmentation is the pulling to pieces (the tearing) of that which never has preexisted (really or ideally) as a whole, nor can it ever be reassembled in any future presence whatever. Fragmentation is the spacing, the separation effected by a temporalization which can only be understood—fallaciously—as the absence of time.

♦ The fragment, as fragments, tends to dissolve the totality which it presupposes and which it carries off toward the dissolution from which it does not (properly speaking) form, but to which it exposes itself in order, disappearing—and along with it, all identity—to maintain itself as the energy of disappearing: a repetitive energy, the limit that bears upon limitation — or the presence of the work of art's absence (to say it all again and to silence by saying it again). So it is that the travesty of the System — the System raised by irony to an absolute of absoluteness — is a way for the System still to impose itself by the discredit with which the demand of the fragmentary credits it.

◆ The fragmentary imperative signals to the System which it dismisses (just as it dismisses, in principle, the I, the author) and also ceaselessly invokes, just as the *other* term in an alternative cannot altogether ignore the first term which it requires in order to substitute itself. The correct criticism of the System does not consist (as is most often, complacently, supposed) in finding fault with it, or in interpreting it insufficiently (which even Heidegger sometimes does), but rather in rendering it invincible, invulnerable to criticism or, as they say, inevitable. Then, since nothing escapes it because of its omnipresent unity and the perfect cohesion of everything, there remains no place for fragmentary writing unless it come into focus as the impossible necessary: as that which is written in the time outside time, in the sheer suspense which without restraint breaks the seal of unity by, precisely, not breaking it, but by leaving it aside without this abandon's ever being able to be known. It is thus, inasmuch as it separates itself from the manifest, that fragmentary writing does not belong to the One. And thus, again, it denounces thought as experience (in whatever sense this word be taken), no less than thought as the realization of the whole.

◆ *"To have a system, this is what is fatal for the mind; not to have one, this too is fatal. Whence the necessity to observe, while abandoning, the two requirements at once."* (Fr. Schlegel.)

◆ What Schlegel says of philosophy is true for writing: you can only become a writer, you can never be one; no sooner are you, than you are no longer, a writer.

♦ All beauty lies in details: so Valéry said, approximately. But this would be true only if there were an art of details that would no longer have the art of the whole for its context.

♦ The disadvantage (or advantage) of all necessary skepticism is that it raises the hurdle for certitude, or for truth or belief, higher and higher. One comes to believe in nothing through a need to believe in too much and because one still believes too much when one believes in nothing.

♦ How absurd it would be to address this question to the writer: are you a writer through and through? In everything you are, have you yourself become writing—vital and activating? This would be to condemn the writer to death or foolishly to deliver his funeral eulogy.

♦ The fragmentary imperative calls upon us to sense that there is as yet nothing fragmentary, not properly speaking, but improperly speaking.

♦ Affirmation does without proof, provided it claims to prove nothing.

♦ I seek him who would say no. For to say no is to *say* with the brilliance which the "no" is destined to preserve.

♦ What happens through writing is not of the order of things that happen. But in that case, who permits you to claim that anything like writing ever does happen? Or is it that writing is not such that it need ever happen?

♦ Someone (Clavel) has written of Socrates that we have all killed him. Such a statement is not very Socratic. Socrates would not have liked to declare us guilty of anything, or even to hold us responsible for an event which his irony, by urging us not to take it seriously, had in advance rendered insignificant—indeed, beneficent. But, of course, Socrates forgot just one thing: that no one after him could be

Socrates, and that his death killed irony. It is irony that his judges all had it in for; it is irony that we, his just mourners, continue to resent.

◆ Un-knowledge is not a lack of knowledge; it is not even knowledge of the lack but rather that which is hidden by knowledge and ignorance alike: the neutral, the un-manifest.

◆ A "discovery" which one mulls over repeatedly becomes the discovery of this futile rumination.

◆ R.C.[16] is so much a poet that after him poetry shines like a fact, but he is such a poet that after this fact of poetry all facts become questions and even poetic questions.

◆ Fervent commitment to infinite progress is valid only as fervor, since the infinite is the end, precisely, of all progress.

◆ Granted, Hegel is the mortal enemy of Christianity, but this is the case exactly to the extent that he is a Christian: far from being satisfied with a single Mediation (Christ), he makes everything into mediation. Judaism is the sole thought that does not mediate. And that is why Hegel, and Marx, are anti-Judaic, not to say anti-Semitic.

◆ A philosopher who would write as a poet would be aiming for his own destruction. And even so, he could not reach it. Poetry is a question for philosophy which claims to provide it with an answer, and thus to comprehend it (know it). Philosophy, which puts everything into question, is tripped up by poetry, which is the question that eludes it.[17]

◆ Whoever writes is exiled from writing, which is the country — his own — where he is not a prophet.

◆ A person who is not interested in himself is not, for all that, disinterested. He would only begin to be disinterested if the indifference in him about himself had not always already opened him to the other, whom no interest at all can reach.

♦ To write one's autobiography, in order either to confess or to engage in self-analysis, or in order to expose oneself, like a work of art, to the gaze of all, is perhaps to seek to survive, but through a perpetual suicide—a death which is total inasmuch as fragmentary. To write (of) oneself is to cease to be, in order to confide in a guest—the other, the reader—entrusting yourself to him who will henceforth have as an obligation, and indeed as a life, nothing but your inexistence.

♦ In a sense, the "I" cannot be lost, because it does not belong to itself. It only is, therefore, as not its own, and therefore as always already lost.

♦ The mortal leap of the writer without which he would not write is necessarily an illusion to the extent that, in order really to be accomplished, it must not take place.

♦ Given that one can, in a textbook fashion, say: the God of Leibniz is because he is possible, then it is clear that one can likewise say the opposite: the real is real inasmuch as it excludes possibility—because, in other words, it is impossible. The same can be said of death and, still more accurately, of the writing of the disaster.

♦ Only a finite I (a self having finitude for its sole destiny), necessarily comes to recognize, in the other, its responsibility for the infinite.

♦ It is only inasmuch as I am infinite that I am limited.

♦ If, as Levinas affirms, religion is etymologically that which binds, that which holds together, then what of the non-bond which disjoins beyond unity—which escapes the synchrony of "holding together," yet does so without breaking all relations or without ceasing, in this break or in this absence of relation, to open yet another relation? Must one be nonreligious for that?

♦ Infinite-limited, is it you?

♦ If you listen to the "times," you will learn that they tell you in a low voice not to speak in their name, but to be silent in their name.

♦ Granted, Socrates does not write; but, beneath the voice, it is nevertheless through writing that he gives himself to others as the perpetual subject perpetually destined to die. He does not speak; he questions. Questioning, he interrupts and interrupts himself without cease, giving form ironically to the fragmentary; through his death, he causes speech to be haunted by writing, and likewise limits writing to a single form: that of the testament (without any signature, though).

♦ Between the two falsely interrogative propositions — why is there something rather than nothing? and, why is there evil rather than good? — I do not recognize the difference which is supposed to be discernible, for both are sustained by a "there is" [*un "il y a"*] which is neither being nor nothingness, neither good nor evil, and without which the whole discussion collapses, or on account of which it has already collapsed. Above all, the *il y a,* because neutral, mocks the questions which bear upon it: when interrogated, it ironically absorbs the inquiry which cannot oversee it. Even if it lets itself be vanquished, it does so because defeat is its disadvantageous advantage, just as the bad infinitude of its endless repetition determines it as true to the extent that it (falsely) imitates transcendence, thus exposing the essential ambiguity of transcendence and the impossibility that this ambiguity be measured according to truth or legitimacy.

♦ Dying means: you are dead already, in an immemorial past, of a death which was not yours, which you have thus neither known nor lived, but under the threat of which you believe you are called upon to live; you await it henceforth in the future, constructing a future to make it possible at last — possible as something that will take place and will belong to the realm of experience.

To write is no longer to situate death in the future — the death which is always already past; to write is to accept that one has to die without making death present and without making oneself present to it. To write is to know that death has taken place even though it has not been experienced, and to recognize it in the forgetfulness that it leaves — in the traces which, effacing themselves, call upon one to *exclude oneself from the cosmic order* and to abide where the disaster makes the real impossible and desire undesirable.

This uncertain death, always anterior — this vestige of a past that never has been present — is never individual; likewise it exceeds the whole (and thus presupposes the fulfillment of the whole, its realization, the endless end of the dialectic). Outside of the whole, of time, this doubtful death cannot be explained, as Winnicott would have it, simply by the vicissitudes characteristic of earliest childhood, when the child, still deprived of a self, is subject to overwhelming states (primitive agonies) which he cannot know since he does not yet exist, which happen thus without taking place and later lead the adult, in a memory without memory and through his fissured self, to expect them (either with desire or with dread) from his life when it ends, from the collapse of his existence. Or rather, this understanding of Winnicott's is only an explanation, albeit impressive — a fictive application designed to individualize that which cannot be individualized or to furnish a representation for the unrepresentable: to allow the belief that one can, with the help of the transference, fix in the present of a memory (that is, in a present experience) the passivity of the immemorial unknown. The introduction of such a detour is perhaps therapeutically useful, to the extent that, through a kind of platonism, it permits him who lives haunted by the imminent collapse to say: this will not happen, it has already happened; I know, I remember. It allows him to restore, in other words, a knowledge which is a relation to truth, and a common, linear temporality.

◆ If it weren't for prisons, we would know that we are all already in prison.

◆ Impossible necessary death: why do these words—and the experience to which they refer (the inexperience)—escape comprehension? Why this collision of mutually exclusive terms? Why efface them by considering them as a fiction peculiar to some particular author? It is only natural. Thought cannot welcome that which it bears within itself and which sustains it, except by forgetting. I will speak soberly of it, using (perhaps falsifying) the impressive remarks of Serge Leclaire. According to him, one lives and speaks only by killing the *infans* in oneself (in others also); but what is the infans? Obviously, that in us which has not yet begun to speak and never will speak; but, more importantly, the marvelous (terrifying) child which we have been in the dreams and the desires of those who were present at our birth (parents, society in general). Where is this child? According to psychoanalytic vocabulary (which, I believe, only those who practice psychoanalysis can use—only those, that is, for whom analysis is a risk, an extreme danger, a daily test—for otherwise it is only the convenient language of an established culture), according, then, to psychoanalytic vocabulary, one might identify the child with "primary narcissistic representation," which is to say that this representation has the status of an ever-unconscious, and consequently, forever indelible, representation. Whence the literally "maddening" difficulty: in order not to remain in the limbo of the infans, on the near side of desire, one must destroy the indestructible and even finish off (not at one blow, but constantly) that to which one has not now, nor has one ever had, nor will one ever have, access: impossible, necessary death. And once again, we live and speak (but with what sort of speech?) only because death has already taken place: an unsituated, unsituatable event which, lest we become mute in very speech, we entrust to the work of the concept (negativity), or again to the psychoanalytic work which cannot but lift and relieve us of "the ordinary confusion" between this first death which would be an interminable accomplishment and the second death which is called, in a facile simplification, "organic" (as if the first were not).

But in all this we are questioning and we are remembering the steps Hegel took: can the confusion — what is termed confusion — ever be dissipated otherwise than by a sleight of hand, the ruse (conveniently) called idealist, whose significance is naturally of great importance? Yes, let us remember the earliest Hegel. He too, even prior to his "early" philosophy, considered that the two deaths were indissociable, and that only the act of confronting death — not merely of facing it or of exposing oneself to its danger (which is the distinguishing feature of heroic courage), but of entering into its space, of undergoing it as infinite death and also as mere death, "natural death" — could found the sovereignty of masterhood: the mind and its prerogatives. The result was perhaps, absurdly, that the experience which initiates the movement of the dialectic — the experience which none experiences, the experience of death — stopped it right away, and that the entire subsequent process retained a sort of memory of this halt, as if of an aporia which always had still to be accounted for. I will not go into detail about the way in which, from Hegel's early philosophy onward, and through the prodigious enrichment of his thought, the difficulty was surmounted. This is well known. It remains, however, that if death, murder, suicide are put to work, and if death loses its sting by becoming powerless power and then negativity, there is, each time one advances with the help of *possible* death, the necessity not to advance any further, not to approach the death without expression, the death without any name, the death outside the concept — *impossibility* itself.

I will add a remark, or rather, a question. Serge Leclaire's child, the glorious, terrifying, tyrannical infans, whom one cannot kill because one only accedes to life and to the possibility of speech by never ceasing to consign him to death — would this child not be Winnicott's? The child who, before living, has sunk into dying? The dead child whom no awareness, no experience can ever define as past history and thus leave behind? Glorious is this child, and terrifying, and tyrannical, because without our knowing it (even and especially when we pretend to know and to say it, as is the case here), he is always already dead. What we strive thus to kill is the dead child: not only the one who would have for his function to sustain and maintain death in life, but the one for whom the "confusion" of the two deaths has been unable not to obtain and who, therefore, does not ever authorize us to "lift" this confusion—who renders the *Aufhebung* null and void, and vain all refutations of suicide.

I observe that Serge Leclaire and Winnicott strive, in almost the same way, to avert us from suicide by showing that it is no solution. Nothing could be more correct. If death is the infinite patience of that which is never accomplished once and for all, then suicide's shortcut necessarily fails death, for it "seems" to transform that which cannot take place because it has always already done so, into an active possibility. But perhaps suicide should be considered differently.

It is possible that suicide is the way in which the unconscious (the wake, the vigilance of what cannot awaken), warns us that something rings false in the dialectic, by reminding us that the child always still to be killed is the child already dead and that thus, in suicide—in what we call suicide—*nothing at all happens.* Whence the feeling of incredulity, or fright, which suicide always provokes in us, at the same time that it incites the desire to refute it, that is, to make it real, which is to say, impossible. The "nothing happens" of suicide can perfectly well take on the form of an event in a story which thereby—by this bold end (the apparent result of purposeful initiative)—displays an individual *bent*: but the enigma is precisely that in killing myself, "I" do not kill "me," but, giving away the secret as it were, someone (or something) uses a vanishing me—as a figure for an Other—the better to reveal to him, and to all, what immediately escapes: the belatedness of death, the immemorial past of ancient death. There is no death now or in the future (no death whose present is to come). Suicide is perhaps—it is no doubt—a fraud, but it has for its stakes to make for an instant evident—hidden—the other fraud which is the death known as organic or natural, and which is fraudulent to the extent that it claims to present itself as distinct, definitively separate and not to be confounded, able to take place, and to take place only once, like that banality, the utterly unique, the unthinkable.

But what would the difference be between death by suicide and death by any other cause (if there is such a thing)? The difference is that the first, by entrusting itself to the dialectic (entirely founded upon the *possibility* of death, upon the use of death as power) is the obscure oracle which we do not decipher, but thanks to which we sense, and ceaselessly forget, that he who has been all the way to the end of the desire of death, invoking his right to death and exerting over himself a power of death, he who opens, as Heidegger said, *the possibility of impossibility*—or again, he who believes himself to be master of un-mastery—lets himself get caught in a sort of trap and halts eternally (halts, obviously, just an instant) at the point where, ceasing to be a subject, losing his stubborn liberty, and becoming other than himself, he comes up against death as that which doesn't happen or as that which reverses itself (betraying, as though demented, the mendacity of the dialectic by bringing it to its conclusion)—reverses the possibility of impossibility into *the impossibility of every possibility*.

Suicide is in a sense a demonstration (whence its arrogant, hurtful, indiscreet character), and what it demonstrates is the undemonstrable: that in death nothing comes to pass and that death itself does not pass (whence the vanity and the necessity of its repetitiveness). But from this aborted demonstration there remains the following: that we die "naturally," of the death that requires no fuss and is of no note conceptually (this affirmation is always to be put into doubt), only if, through a constant, an inapparent and *preliminary* suicide, accomplished by no one, we encounter (of course, it is not "we") the semblance of the end of history, when everything returns to nature (a nature which is supposed to be denatured), and when death, ceasing to be an always double death, having apparently exhausted the infinite passivity of dying, reduces itself to the simplicity of something natural, more insignificant and more uninteresting than the collapse of a little heap of sand.

♦ "A child is being killed." This is the title which must at last be recalled in all its indecisive force. It is not I who would have to kill and always to kill again the infans that I was, so to speak, in the beginning and when I was not yet, but was at least in the dreams, the desires and the imaginary of some, and then of all. There is death and murder (words which I defy anyone seriously to distinguish and which must nonetheless be separated); but there is no designated or designatable dealer of death. It is an impersonal, inactive, and irresponsible "they" that must answer for this death and this murder. And likewise this child is a child, but one who is always undetermined and without relation to anyone at all. A child already dead is dying, of a murderous death — a child of whom we know nothing (even if we characterize him as marvelous, terrifying, tyrannical, or indestructible) except this: that the possibility of speaking and of life depend on the fictive establishment, through death and murder, of a relation of singularity with a mute past, with a prehistory, with a past, then, which is outside the past and of which the eternal infans is the figure at the same time that he is concealed therein. "A child is being killed." Let us make no mistake about this present: it signifies that the deed cannot be done once and for all, that the operation is completed at no privileged moment in time — that, in-operable, it operates and that thus it tends to be none but the very time which destroys (effaces) time. This is the effacement or destruction, or gift, which has always already been exposed in the precession of Speaking — Speaking separate from and outside of anything spoken, the sheer saying of writing — whereby this effacement, far from effacing itself in its turn, perpetuates itself without end, even in the interruption that is its mark.

"A child is being killed." This silent passive, this dead eternity to which a temporal form of life must be given in order that we might separate ourselves from it by a murder — this companion, but of no one, whom we seek to particularize as an absence, that we might live upon his banishment, desire with the desire he has not, and speak through and against the word he does not utter — nothing (neither knowledge nor un-knowledge) can designate him, even if the simplest of sentences seems, in four or five words, to divulge him (a child is being killed). But this sentence is immediately torn from language — from every language in which it is articulated — for it draws us outside consciousness and unconsciousness each time we pronounce it: each time it is given us, that is — other than ourselves and in a relation of impossibility with the other — to pronounce the unpronounceable.

♦ (A primal scene?) *You who live later, close to a heart that beats no more, suppose, suppose this: the child — is he seven years old, or eight perhaps? — standing by the window, drawing the curtain and, through the pane, looking. What he sees: the garden, the wintry trees, the wall of a house. Though he sees, no doubt in a child's way, his play space, he grows weary and slowly looks up toward the ordinary sky, with clouds, grey light — pallid daylight without depth.*

What happens then: the sky, the same sky, suddenly open, absolutely black and absolutely empty, revealing (as though the pane had broken) such an absence that all has since always and forevermore been lost therein — so lost that therein is affirmed and dissolved the vertiginous knowledge that nothing is what there is, and first of all nothing beyond. The unexpected aspect of this scene (its interminable feature) is the feeling of happiness that straightaway submerges the child, the ravaging joy to which he can bear witness only by tears, an endless flood of tears. He is thought to suffer a childish sorrow; attempts are made to console him. He says nothing. He will live henceforth in the secret. He will weep no more.

♦ Something rings false in the dialectic, but only the dialectical process, in its inexhaustible demand, in its ever-maintained completion, allows us to think what is excluded from it — not on account of weakness or because it is unacceptable, but in the course of the process's functioning and in order that this functioning be interminably pursued all the way to its term. All the way, that is, to the end of history: the world completely known and totally transformed, in the unity of the knowledge which knows itself (and this is to say that the world has forever *become,* or that it is *dead,* like man, who was its temporary representation, like the Subject whose sage identity is no longer anything but indifference to life, life's immobile vacancy). At that point, where it is given us on the rare occasion—albeit fictively and by the most dangerous stratagem—to convey ourselves, we are by no means freed from the dialectic, but it becomes pure Discourse: that which speaks, utters itself and says nothing, the Book which destroys by constructing itself, the work of the "No" in its multiple forms behind which reading, and writing, prepare for the advent of a "Yes" both unique and ever reiterated in the circularity where there is no longer any first and last affirmation.

We might well imagine that we are at that point: whence our concern for language; whence the theory-practice of language independently of which it seems no knowledge can henceforth suggest itself. It is as if the reversal which Marx proposed with regard to Hegel—"to pass from language to life"—had in turn been reversed, and life, having been finished off (that is to say, fully realized), were restoring to a language without referent (which thereby becomes the science of itself and the model of all science) the task of saying everything by saying itself endlessly. This hypothesis can, while appearing to disown the dialectic, serve to prolong it in other forms, so that one would never be sure that the dialectical imperative does not aspire to its own renunciation only in order to renew itself from what renders it obsolete, ineffective. Whence it follows—but perhaps nothing follows, not even this perhaps, nor that we are condemned always to be saved by the dialectic. For first it must be ascertained what authorizes the doubt that the dialectic can ever be, I wouldn't say refuted (the possibility of a refutation is part of its development), but simply refused. And if the doubt is unauthorized and does not succeed in wrecking the refusal, then it must be explained why the refusal would not be the initial one—the refusal to begin, the refusal to philosophize, to enter into a dialogue with Socrates, or, more generally, to prefer violence that is already speaking to mute violence. Without this preference or choice, there could be, according to Eric Weil, neither dialectic nor philosophy, nor knowledge. Or does something of the refusal remain, perhaps, in the dialectical process? Would it not persist, all the while modifying itself, until it gives place to something one might call a non-dialectic imperative? Or better, could what rings false in the dialectic and yet makes it function ever separate itself from the dialectic? Under what conditions, at what cost? That the cost would be high, very high — that the cost would no doubt be reason, in the form of the logos (but is there any other form?) — this we can foresee. And — another presentiment — if there are limits to the realm of the dialectic, since these displace themselves ceaselessly, one must abandon the naive belief that one might, once and for all, cross those limits, designate zones of knowledge and of writing which would remain decidedly foreign to the dialectic. But yet again, let us consider whether it is not by attending to the refusal that accompanies it and alters and consolidates it — let us wonder if it is not by obstinately playing its own game — that we might come to outplay the dialectic or to defeat it in its very inability to fail.

In the place of the refusal — which is without a place — invoked by Eric Weil, we should perhaps, while keeping well outside of mysticism, hear what we hear not: the undemanding, the disastrous demand of the neutral — the effraction of the infinitely passive where undesirable desire and the push of deathless dying meet, parting.

♦ If someone pronounces this word, the *disaster,* we feel that it is not a word, not the name of anything; indeed, we feel that there never is a separate, nominal, predominant name, but always an entire complex or simple sentence, where the infinitude of language — of language in its unfinished history and its unclosed system — seeks to let itself be taken in hand by a sequence of verbs, and yet seeks at the same time, in the never resolved tension between noun and verb, to fall, as if immobilized, outside language—without, however, ceasing to belong to it.

Thus does the patience of the disaster lead us to expect nothing of the "cosmic" and perhaps nothing of the world, or, on the contrary, very much of the world, if we succeed in disengaging it from the idea of order, of regularity guaranteed by law. For the "disaster," a rip forever ripping apart, seems to say to us: there is not, to begin with, law, prohibition, and then transgression, but rather there is transgression in the absence of any prohibition, which eventually freezes into Law, the Principle of Meaning. The long, the interminable sentence of the disaster: this is what seeks, forming an enigma, to be written, in order to separate us (not once and for all) from the unitary imperative which is necessarily always at work. Is the cosmic the way the sacred, disguising itself as transcendence, seeks to become immanent? Is the cosmic thus the temptation to melt into the fiction of the universe, and thereby become indifferent to the tormenting vicissitudes of the near at hand (the neighboring)? Would the cosmic be a little heaven in which to survive, or with which to die universally, in stoic serenity? A "whole" which shelters us, even as we dissolve therein, and which would be natural repose—as if there were a nature outside of concepts and names?

The disaster: break with the star, break with every form of totality, never denying, however, the dialectical necessity of a fulfillment; the disaster: prophecy which announces nothing but the refusal of the prophetic as simply an event to come, but which nonetheless opens, nonetheless discovers the patience of vigilant language. The disaster, touch of the powerless infinite: it does not come to pass under a sidereal sky, but here—a here in excess of all presence. Here: where, then? *"Voice of no one, once more."*

◆ Theories are necessary (the theories of language, for example): necessary and useless. Reason works in order to wear itself out, by organizing itself into systems, seeking a positive knowledge where it can posit itself, pose and repose and at the same time convey itself to an extremity which forms a stop and closure. We must pass by way of this knowledge and forget it. But forgetting is not secondary; it is not an improvised failing of what has first been constituted as memory. Forgetfulness is a practice, the practice of writing that prophesies because it is enacted by the utter renunciation of everything: to announce is perhaps to renounce. The theoretical battle, even if it is waged against some form of violence, is always the violence of an incomprehension; let us not be stopped short by the partial, simplifying, reductive character of comprehension itself. This partialness is characteristic of the theoretical: "with hammer blows," Nietzsche said. But this hammering is not only the clash of arms. Hammering reason is in search of its last blow, the one that marks the beginning — the end, we know not — of the thought that lasts like a dream in waking hours. Why is skepticism, even when refuted, invincible? Levinas wonders. Hegel knew — Hegel, who made skepticism a privileged moment of the system. This was only to make it serve. Writing too, even if it seems too exposed to be called skeptical, presupposes skepticism's having already and once more cleared everything away in advance, which cannot be done yet, if not by writing.

◆ Skepticism, a noun that has crossed out its etymology and all etymology, is not indubitable doubt; it is not simply nihilist negation: rather, irony. Skepticism is in relation with the refutation of skepticism. We refute it, if only by living, but death does not confirm it. Skepticism is indeed the return of the refuted, that which erupts anarchically, capriciously, and irregularly each time (and at the same time not each time) that authority and the sovereignty of reason, indeed of unreason, impose their order upon us or organize themselves definitively in a system. Skepticism does not destroy the system; it destroys nothing; it is a sort of gaiety without laughter, in any case without mockery, which suddenly makes us uninterested in affirmation, in negation: thus it is neutral like all language. The disaster would be that portion of skeptical gaiety, never at anyone's disposal, that makes seriousness (the seriousness of death, for example) pass beyond all seriousness, just as it lightens the theoretical by not letting us trust it. I recall Levinas: *"Language is in itself already skepticism."*

♦ Tensions that are not resolvable cannot accommodate any affirmation either. Thus one cannot say, as though thereby one freed oneself once and for all from dialectical processes: affirmation of tensions. One should rather say: tense patience, patience unto impatience. The continuous, the discontinuous would seem to be the hyperbolic conflict which we always reencounter, after getting shut of it. Continuity bears within itself the discontinuity which nevertheless excludes it. The continuous imposes itself in all forms, as does the Same. Whence homogeneous time, whence eternity, whence the logos which assembles, whence the order where all change is regulated, and the satisfaction of comprehension, the primacy of the law. But it does not suffice, in order to interrupt the continuity of the continuous, to introduce the heterogeneous (heteronomy). For the latter depends upon the former and forms a compromise with it inasmuch as the interaction between the two is a form of tranquilized opposition that permits life, and includes death. (As when Heraclitus is quoted—complacently and without any sense of what was decided for him by this abrupt way of speaking: "To live on death, to die of life." The translation here takes from the original what there would have been to translate, but does not translate, as is practically always the case.)

Is there a discontinuity imperative that would owe nothing to the continuous—that would not even presuppose in order to interrupt continuity? Why this monotonous torment which is rhythmically articulated in fragmentary writing and which appeals to patience but not because patience would help it narcissistically to endure? Patience without duration, without sequence, indecisive interruption without any point of interest. . . . There the neutral would ceaselessly keep watch without our knowing, in the *tense* failing of an identity — the failing that exposes the subjectivity which is without any subject.

♦ The present, when heightened as successive instants (appearing, disappearing), forgets that it cannot be contemporaneous with itself. This noncontemporaneity is a passage already passed over; it is the passive which, outside time, disarranges time as pure and empty form wherein all would order and distribute itself either equally or unequally. Time that is deranged and off its hinges still lets itself be drawn — if only through the experience of the crack — into a coherence which unifies and universalizes itself. But the experience of the disaster — the experience none can have, the retreat of the cosmic which it is too easy to unmask as utter collapse (the lack of foundation where once and for all, without ambiguity or questions, everything we can conceive of and think would be immobilized) — obliges us to disengage ourselves from time as irreversible, without the Return's assuring its reversibility.

♦ The crack: a fissure which would be constitutive of the self, or would reconstitute itself as the self, but not as a cracked self.

♦ Criticism is almost always important, even if it omits and misrepresents a great deal. However, when straight-away, it becomes warlike, this is because political impatience has won out over the patience proper to the "poetic." Writing, since it persists in a relation of irregularity with itself — and thus with the utterly other — does not know what will become of it politically: this is its intransitivity, its necessarily indirect relation to the political.

This *indirection,* the infinite detour which we try to understand as writing's being, so to speak, out of phase or belated — as incertitude or chance (and also as invention) — makes us unhappy. We would like to proceed in a straightforward way toward the goal — the social transformation which it is in our power to affirm. Some time ago, this impulse was expressed as a desire for active commitment (engagement); to this day it animates the wish for a passionate morality. It is thus that we always manage to consider ourselves divided: on the one hand, there is the free subject, working for his own creative freedom through the struggle for the freedom of everyone; on the other hand, there is the other, who is no longer *one* but always several and, more than that, linked to the plurality which adds up to no total at all, which knows nothing of unity. Too easily—through negative, ambivalent, juxtaposed terms (such as disappearance, separation, dispersion, or such as the nameless, the selfless)—we delimit the difficulty which this other introduces into all efforts to escape our present circumstances. But the language of writing *momentarily,* in the extenuatedness it presupposes—in its repetitive difference, its patient effraction—opens or offers itself in the direction of the other, through very perplexity. It is divided in two that we live-speak, but since the other is always other, we can neither console nor comfort ourselves with the binary choice. And the relation of one to the other ceaselessly comes apart; it undoes every model and every code; it is the nonrelation from which we are not excused.

In the first perspective, "to live—to write—to speak" is given as homogeneous, as if the vicissitudes—the historical vicissitudes—of the single but conflictual relation which these united and separate verbs sustain produced a subject common to all three though always at odds with itself—produced this subject in the realm where it is necessary to act and where language becomes action, in the violent tumult that develops from language and also dominates it. Such is the law of the Same. We must not turn away from it, or stop at it either; and it is thus toward another sort of language entirely—the language of writing, the language of the other always other whose imperative does not develop at all—it is in the direction of this other language that, outside of everything, outside consciousness and unconsciousness, in the element that vacillates between waking and reawaking, we know ourselves (not knowing this) to be always already deported.

Of course, the separation, which seems to affect the one and the other and divide them infinitely, can in its turn give place to a dialectical process. But the other demand — the other of all demands which demands nothing, which always lets itself be excluded: the indelible effacement — is not thereby annulled. It cannot be disposed of by any process or system.

♦ It is through reverence that the work, always already in ruins, is frozen: through reverence which prolongs, maintains, consecrates it (through the idolatry proper to titles), it congeals, or is added to the catalogue of the good works of culture.

♦ And one more word: shouldn't we have done with theory to the extent that it does not ever get over and done, and also to the extent that all theories, however different they may be, constantly change places with one another, distinct each from the next only because of the writing which supports them and which thus escapes the very theories purporting to judge it?

♦ I will consider (as an idea) that the golden age would be the age of despotism, when natural happiness, natural time — that is to say, nature — is perceived in forgetfulness of the Sovereignty of the supreme King, the sole wielder of Truth-Justice who has always put all that is — all things, living beings, humans — in *good order*. This order, then, to which all — that they might live, that they might die — happily submit, is the most natural thing, since rigorous obedience to the government which ensures it effectively makes this government the only one conceivable; it becomes invisible and perfectly secure. Whence it may be concluded that every return to nature is liable to be the nostalgic return to the rule of a single tyrant, or that, if one reads carefully a certain Greek tradition, there is no nature at all and everything is "political" (Gilles Suson). Even according to Aristotle, it is Pisistrates' tyranny which, in the tradition of the Athenian peasantry, was held to be the age of Chronos or the golden age, as if the most rigid hierarchy — when all values are on one side only and are affirmed invisibly, unconditionally — were the equivalent of an alluring trap.

♦ The suffering of our time: *"A wasted man, bent head, bowed shoulders, unthinking, gaze extinguished." "Our gaze was turned to the ground."*

♦ Concentration camps, annihilation camps, emblems wherein the invisible has made itself visible forever. All the distinctive features of a civilization are revealed or laid bare ("Work liberates," "rehabilitation through work"). Work, in societies where, indeed, it is highly valued as the materialist process whereby the worker takes power, becomes the ultimate punishment: no longer is it just a matter of exploitation or of surplus-value; labor becomes the point at which all value comes to pieces and the "producer," far from reproducing at least his labor force, is no longer even the reproducer of his life. For work has ceased to be his way of living and has become his way of dying. Work, death: equivalents. And the workplace is everywhere; worktime is all the time. When oppression is absolute, there is no more leisure, no more "free time." Sleep is supervised. The meaning of work is then the destruction of work in and through work. But what if, as it has happened in certain commandos, labor consists of carrying stones at top speed from one spot and piling them up in another, and then in bringing them back at the run to the starting point (Langbein at Auschwitz; the same episode in the Gulag; Solzhenitsyn)? Then, no act of sabotage can cancel work, for its annulment is work's own very purpose. And yet labor retains a meaning: it tends not only to destroy the worker, but more immediately to occupy, to harness and control him and at the same time perhaps to give him an awareness that to produce and not to produce amount to the same — that the one and the other alike are work — yet thereby it also makes the worker, whom it reduces to naught, aware that the society expressed in the labor camp is what he must struggle against even as he dies, even as he survives (lives on despite everything, beneath everything, beyond everything). Such

survival is (also) immediate death, immediate acceptance of death in
the refusal to die (I will not kill myself, because that would please
them; thus I kill myself opposing them, I remain alive despite
them).

♦ Knowledge which goes so far as to accept horror in order to know
it, reveals the horror of knowledge, its squalor, the discrete complic-
ity which maintains it in a relation with the most insupportable
aspects of power. I think of that young prisoner of Auschwitz (he
had suffered the worst, led his family to the crematorium, hanged
himself; after being saved at the last moment—how can one say
that: *saved?*—he was exempted from contact with dead bodies, but
when the SS shot someone, he was obliged to hold the victim's head
so that the bullet could be more easily lodged in the neck). When
asked how he could bear this, he is supposed to have answered that
he "observed the comportment of men before death." I will not believe it. As Lewental, whose notes were found buried near a crematorium, wrote to us, "The truth was always more atrocious, more
tragic than what will be said about it." Saved at the last minute, the
young man of whom I speak was forced to live that last instant again
and each time to live it once more, frustrated every time of his own
death and made to exchange it every time for the death of all. His
response ("I observed the comportment of men . . . ") was not a response; he could not respond. What remains for us to recognize in
this account is that when he was faced with an impossible question,
he could find no other alibi than the search for knowledge, the so-
called dignity of knowledge: that ultimate propriety which we believe will be accorded us by knowledge. And how, in fact, can one
accept not to know? We read books on Auschwitz. The wish of all,
in the camps, the last wish: know what has happened, do not forget,
and at the same time never will you know.

♦ Can one say: horror reigns at Auschwitz, senselessness in the
Gulag? Horror, because extermination in every form is the immediate horizon. Zombies, pariahs, infidels: such is the truth of life.

However, a certain number resist; the word "political" retains a meaning; there must be survivors to bear witness, perhaps to win. In the Gulag, until the death of Stalin and except for members of the political opposition about whom memorialists say little—too little (except Joseph Berger)—no one is political. No one knows why he is there. Resistance has no meaning, if not simply for oneself, or for the sake of friendship, which is rare. Only the religious have firm convictions capable of giving significance to life, and to death. Thus resistance is spiritual. Not until the revolts issuing from the depths, and then the dissidents and their clandestine writings, do perspectives open—do ruined words become audible rising from the ruins, traversing the silence.

Surely, senselessness is at Auschwitz, horror in the Gulag. Nonsense at its most derisory is best represented (perhaps) by the son of the Lagerfürher Schwarzhuber. At ten years old, he sometimes came to fetch his father at the camp. One day, he couldn't be found, and right away his father thought: he's gotten swept up by mistake and thrown with the others into the gas chamber. But the child had only been hiding, and thereafter he was made to wear a placard for identification purposes. Another sign is Himmler's fainting at mass executions. And the consequence: fearing he'd shown weakness, he gave the order to multiply the executions, and gas chambers were invented: death humanized on the outside. Inside was horror at its most extreme. Or again, sometimes concerts were organized. The power of music seems, momentarily, to bring forgetfulness and dangerously causes the distance between murderers and victims to disappear. But, Langbein adds, for the pariahs there was neither sport nor music. There is a limit at which the practice of any art becomes an affront to affliction. Let us not forget this.

♦ We must still meditate (but is it possible?) upon this: in the camp, if (as Robert Antelme said while enduring it) need sustains everything, maintaining an infinite relation to life even if it be in the most abject manner (but here it is no longer a matter of high or

low)—if need consecrates life through an egotism without ego—
there is also the point at which need no longer helps one to live, but
is an aggression against the entire person: a torment which denudes,
an obsession of the whole being whereby the being is utterly destroyed. Dull, extinguished eyes burn suddenly with a savage gleam
for a shred of bread, "even if one is perfectly aware that death is a few
minutes away" and that there is no longer any point in nourishment.
This gleam, this brilliance does not illuminate anything living.
However, with this gaze which is a last gaze, bread is given us as
bread. This gift, outside all reason, and at the point where all values
have been exterminated—in nihilist desolation and when all objective order has been given up—maintains life's fragile chance by the
sanctification of hunger—nothing "sacred," let us understand, but
something which is given without being broken or shared by him
who is dying of it (*"Great is hungering,"* Levinas says, recalling a
Jewish saying). But at the same time the fascination of the dying
gaze, where the spark of life congeals, does not leave intact the
need's demand, not even in a primitive form, for it no longer allows
hunger (it no longer allows bread) to be related in any way to
nourishment. In this ultimate moment when dying is exchanged for
the life of bread, not, any longer, in order to satisfy a need and still
less in order to make bread desirable, need—in need—also dies as
simple need. And it exalts, it glorifies—by making it into something inhuman (withdrawn from all satisfaction)—the need of bread
which has become an empty absolute where henceforth we can all
only ever lose ourselves.

But the danger (here) of words in their theoretical insignificance is
perhaps that they claim to evoke the annihilation where all sinks always, without hearing the "be silent" addressed to those who have
known only partially, or from a distance the interruption of history.
And yet to watch and to wake, to keep the ceaseless vigil over the
immeasurable absence is necessary, for what took up again from this
end (Israel, all of us) is marked by this end, from which we cannot
come to the end of waking again.

◆ If forgetfulness precedes memory or perhaps founds it, or has no connection with it at all, then to forget is not simply a weakness, a failing, an absence or void (the starting point of a recollection but a starting point which, like an anticipatory shade, would obscure remembrance in its very possibility, restoring the memorable to its fragility and memory to the loss of memory). No, forgetfulness would be not emptiness, but neither negative nor positive: the passive demand that neither welcomes nor withdraws the past, but, designating there what has never taken place (just as it indicates in the yet to come that which will never be able to find its place in any present), refers us to nonhistorical forms of time, to the other of all tenses, to their eternal or eternally provisional indecision, bereft of destiny, without presence.

Forgetfulness would efface that which never was inscribed: it would bar the unwritten which thus seems to have left a trace that must be obliterated. And this slippage in the significance of forgetfulness comes to construct for itself an operator: the impersonal third-person, the subject without subjectivity, slick and vain, thickens, acquiring a sort of stickiness, and becomes trapped in the doubled abyss of the evanescent, simulated I, an imitation of nothing, which congeals in the confident Self whence all order returns.

◆ We assume that forgetfulness works in the manner of the negative to restore itself in memory—in a living, revivified memory. This is so. It can be otherwise. But even if we boldly separate forgetfulness from memory, still we seek only an effect of forgetfulness (an effect of which forgetfulness is not the cause)—a sort of hidden elaboration *of* the hidden which would keep separate from the manifest and which, identifying itself with this very separation (nonidentity) and maintaining itself as not-manifest, would nevertheless serve nothing but manifestation. In such a manner does *lèthé* end sadly, gloriously, as *alèthéia*. Inoperative forgetfulness, forever idled, which is nothing and does nothing (and which not even dying would reach): this is what, hiding itself from awareness and from unawareness too, does not leave us alone, nor does it disturb us, for we have covered it over with consciousness-unconsciousness.

♦ Myth would seem to be the radicalization of a hypothesis, the hypothesis whereby thought, going right to the limit, has always included what desimplifies, disjoins, and undoes it, what destroys at its strongest point the possibility of its maintaining itself even through fictional narrative (a return to sheer telling). But the word "myth"—to the extent that without crossing out the word "truth," it offers itself as nontrue—still protects the bygone which will have no effect, at least for those (all of us) who, being alive, seem to recognize only the active power of the present. Likewise, the radicalization whereby etymology's linkages appear to promise us the security of a native habitat is the hiding place of the homelessness which the ultimate's demand (the eschatological imperative: without finality and without logos) incites in us as uprooted creatures, deprived by language itself of language—of language understood as *ground* where the germinal root would plunge, and as the promise of a developing life.

♦ The simplest words convey the inexchangeable; they switch back and forth with each other all around it; it appears not.

Life so precarious: never the presence of life, but our eternal prayer to the other that he might live while we die.

♦ Of mythical or hyperbolic "cancer": why does it frighten us with its name, as if thereby the unnamable were designated? It claims to defeat the coded system under whose auspices, living and accepting to live, we abide in the security of a purely formal existence, obeying a model signal according to a program whose process is apparently perfectly normative. "Cancer" would seem to symbolize (and "realize") the refusal to respond: here is a cell that doesn't hear the command, that develops lawlessly, in a way that could be called anarchic. It does still more: it destroys the very idea of a program, blurring the exchange and the message: it wrecks the possibility of reducing everything to the equivalent of signs. Cancer, from this perspective, is a political phenomenon, one of the rare ways to dislocate the system, to disarticulate, through proliferation and disorder, the universal programming and signifying power. This task was accomplished in other times by leprosy, then by the Plague. Something we cannot understand maliciously neutralizes the authority of a master knowledge. It is thus not simply as death at work that cancer seems so singular a menace; it is as a mortal derangement, a derangement more threatening than the fact of dying, and which gives that fact back its essential trait: its way of not letting itself be accounted for or brought to account, any more than suicide, which disappears from the statistics that are supposed to keep count of it.

♦ Words to avoid because of their excessive theoretical freight: "signifier," "symbolic," "text," "textual," and then "being," and then finally all words, and this would still not suffice, for since words cannot be constituted as a totality, the infinity that traverses them could never be captured by a subtracting operation; it is irreducible by reduction.

♦ Giving voice to the common lot — common not according to being, but according to what is *other* than being, and draws near unordered, unchosen, unwelcomed, the impotence of attraction.

♦ *Calm, always calmer, the undesirable calm.*

♦ In common we have: burdens. Insupportable, immeasurable, unsharable burdens. The community does not secure itself against such disproportion; it has always left behind the mutual exchange from which it seems to come. It is the life of the nonreciprocal, of the inexchangeable — of that which ruins exchange. Exchange always goes by the law of stability. But to change presupposes, in contrast, unchange: a change, that is, stemming from the outside which excludes the mutable and the immutable alike, and also the relation that is introduced surreptitiously with the one and the other.

♦ *There remains the unnamed in the* name *of which we keep still.*

♦ The gift, prodigality, consummation—it is only momentarily that these displace the general system which is dominated by the law, and which itself only barely distinguishes between the useful and the useless. Consummation becomes consumption; the gift is balanced by a rival generosity. Waste is part of the rigorous administration of things which requires a certain slack. It is no longer a sign of failure, but a form of use whereby utility preserves itself by accommodating what is apparently of no use. Thus one cannot speak of loss "pure and simple." Or rather, one cannot speak of anything else, until loss, always inappropriate and impure, reverberates in language as that which never can be said, but resounds infinitely by losing itself therein and by making language attentive to the imperative that it lose itself—a demand which is in itself undemanding or already lost.

Neither the sun, nor the universe helps us, except through images, to conceive of a system of exchanges so marked by loss that nothing therein would hold together and that the inexchangeable would no longer be caught and defined in symbolic terms. (Georges Bataille never thought for very long that "the sun is nothing but death.") The cosmic reassures us, for we can identify with the measureless vibration of a sovereign order even if in this identification we venture beyond ourselves, entrusting ourselves to a holy and real unity. So it is with *being* and probably with all ontology. The thought of being never fails to enclose; it includes even what it cannot take in—its boundlessness is always confirmed by its limits. The language of being is a language which subjects and reverts to being, saying obedience, submission, expressing the sovereign audience of being in its hidden-disclosed presence. The refusal of being is still assent; it is being's consent to refusal. Being grants, to the refusal of possibility, its possibility. In this refusal, defiance of the law can only be declared in the name of the law which thereby is affirmed.

Abandon the futile hope of finding in being the basis for a separation, a break, a revolt that could be achieved, and *verified*. For thus you are still in need of the truth and of putting it above "error," just as you want to distinguish death from life and death from death. Thus you stay loyal to the staunchness of a faith which dares not recognize its emptiness and is content with a transcendence of which *being would still be the measure*. Seek, then — seeking nothing — that which exhausts being exactly where it represents itself as inexhaustible. Seek the vanity of the incessant, the repetitiveness of the interminable where there is perhaps no cause to distinguish to be and not to be, truth and error, death and life, for each refers back to the other, just as similarity deepens into sheer resemblance — resembling nothing, incomparable. Seek the ceaselessness of the return, effect of disastrous instability.

◆ Is the gift an act of sovereignty whereby the "I," giving freely and gratuitously, would waste or destroy "goods"? The sovereign gift is still only the privilege of sovereignty, an enrichment of glory and prestige, even when it is the heroic gift of one's life. But the gift is rather retreat, withdrawal — the uprooting and above all the suspension of oneself. The gift, it seems, is the passive passion which doesn't allow the power of giving, but, deposing me from myself, causes me to owe the very pain that is caused me when I no longer have anything, and *am* no more. It is as if giving marked, in its nearness, the infinite separation — the incommensurable distance of which the other is not so much the farthest point as the undeterminable strangeness. That is why to give is not to give something — even lavishly, asking naught in return. It is neither to dispense something nor to expend oneself. It is rather to give what is always taken, which is perhaps to say time: my time inasmuch as it is never mine, the time which is not at my disposal, the time beyond me and my living particularity, the lapse of time. To give is to give living and dying not at my time but according to the time of the *other,* which is the unrepresentable representation of a time without present and always returning.

◆ Would the gift of time be dissonance with all that is in harmony, loss (in time and because of time) of contemporaneity, of synchrony, of "community" (of that which assembles and gathers together)? Would it be the coming—which does not ever come— of irregularity and instability? While everything keeps going, nothing goes together.

♦ Energy, as destruction of things or as removal from among things, destroys and removes itself. Let us acknowledge this. However, this loss, as the disappearance of things—the disappearance, indeed, of the order of things—seeks in its turn to get into line, either by reinvesting itself as another thing, or by letting itself be spoken. Thereby, thanks to this discourse that makes a theme of it, it becomes considerable, it fits back into order and "consecrates" itself. Only order gains from its loss.

♦ "Sovereignty is NOTHING." (G.B.)[18]

♦ Between the man of faith and the man of science, there is little difference: both guard against destructive chance and reconstitute the requirements of order; both appeal to a constant which they pray to or theorize about; both are men of accommodation and of unity for whom the other and the same are complementary. Speaking, writing, calculating, they are eternal conservers, conservers of eternity, always in quest of something stable, and pronouncing the word "ontological" with confident fervor.

♦ *"Poetry, ladies and gentlemen: an expression of infinitude, an expression of vain death and of mere Nothing."* (Celan). If death is vain, then so too is the expression of death, including the one that believes it says so, and disappoints by saying so.

Do not count on death—on your own or on universal death—to found anything whatsoever, even the reality of this death. For it is so uncertain and so unreal that it always fades away ahead of time, and with it whatever declares it. The two formulations "God is dead," "Man is dead," which are meant to clang loudly in credulous ears,

and which are easily reversed to the profit of all kinds of belief, certainly show (perhaps they show) that transcendence — that word,
that big word which ought to be its own ruination but which retains
a majestic power — always wins out, even if only in a negative form.
Death takes charge of divine transcendence for its own use, in order
to elevate language above and beyond every term. From the death of
God it follows that death is of God. And from there, the imitative
sentence "Man is dead" by no means defeats the word "man," showing man to be a transitory notion, but announces either a super-
humanity (with all its venturesome imitations), or the denunciation
of the human figure — in order that once again, and in its place, the
divine absolute which death not only eliminates but at the same
time ushers in, might be proclaimed.

Whence the necessity that we bear in mind what, ironically
("ladies and gentlemen"), Celan wanted to tell us. Can we? I retain
this at least: that he relates, in a relation of enigmatic juxtaposition,
the expression "infinitude" and the expression "vain death" — the
latter doubled by "Nothing" as its decisive ending: the final
nothingness which nevertheless occupies the same plane (without
either preceding or succeeding it), as the expression which comes
from the infinite, wherein the infinite gives itself and resounds infinitely.

Expression of infinitude, expression of nothing: do these go
together? Yes, but without agreement. Without agreement but
without discord. For there is an expression of the one and of the
other, which suggests that there would be no poetic expression at all
if the infinite accord, the infinite hearing each accords the other, did
not give itself to be heard as the strictly determined resonance of
death in its emptiness. Such a proximity of absence would be the
very trait proper to *giving all*. And so I arrive at this supposition:
"God is dead," "Man is dead" are perhaps — because of the pre-
sumption of that which seeks to affirm itself in these phrases by
treating "being dead" as a possibility of God and likewise a possibil-

ity of man—only the symptom of a language still too powerful, too sovereign as it were, which thus gives up speaking poorly, in vain and forgetfully, gives up failure, indigence, the extinction of the breath. And these are *the sole marks of poetry*. (But, "sole"? This purposefully exclusive word fails poverty, which cannot defend itself, and must in its turn be extinguished.)

♦ One may well be suspicious of a language and of thinking which must have recourse, in different forms, to negative qualifications in order to introduce questions heretofore held in reserve. We investigate un-power, but do we not do so from the vantage point of power? We speak of the impossible, but do we not always say it is the outer limit, or the articulation, of possibility? We surrender to the unconscious, but without succeeding in separating it from consciousness except negatively. We carry on about atheism, which has always been a privileged way of talking about God. Conversely, the infinite extricates itself from the finite only as the latter's incapacity to finish finishing, as its endless pursuit of itself along the ambiguous detour of repetition. Even the absolute, as a massive and solitary affirmation, bears the mark of what it denies, inasmuch as the absolute is the rejection of every solution, the breaking off of every bond and of every relation. Finally, even the stress, in a philosophical or post-philosophical discourse, on the Greek *aléthès,* whose etymological meaning is said to be un-hidden, not-latent, suggests the primacy of the hidden with respect to the manifest, of the latent with respect to the disclosed, so that if one refuses to put the negative to work the way Hegel does, there would be in what would henceforth be called truth, not the primary trait of all that presents itself, but the already secondary privation of something more ancient, of something concealed—of a withdrawal or retreat which is such not with respect to man or in him, and which is not destined to disclosure, but is borne by language as its silent secret. Whence it can be concluded that by studying the etymologies of a given tongue in a necessarily abusive fashion (etymology is, after all, only one type of study), it is also abusively that one will come to privilege the word "presence" understood as being. Not that one ought to say the contrary—that presence would refer back to an always already refused absence, or that presence, the presence of being and as such always true, would simply be a way of warding off lack, or more precisely of failing lack—but that perhaps there is no reason at all to establish a relation of subordination or any relation whatever between absence and presence, and that the "root" of a term, far from being its first sense, its *proper* meaning, only comes to language through a play of interdependent little signs which are by themselves ill-determined or of doubtful significance. These determinants which put indetermination into play (or indeterminants which determine) draw what wants to be said into a general errant drift where there is no longer any term that as meaning would belong to itself and where, for a center, each has but the possibility of being decentered: bent, inflected, exteriorized, denied, or repeated. At the most, lost. (One can still propose this remark for reflection, despite the likelihood of fashion's making off with it to emphasize, as a useful index, that in language which is not indicated—repetitive neutralization.)

◆ Etymology, or a mode of thought authorized by, or elaborated through etymological considerations, opens a realm of questions which it seems, however, to neglect, as if prejudices we are unwilling or unable to recognize were what attracted us to etymology. The word "etymology" itself refers through its etymology to an affirmation that defines the object of etymological investigations: it is the science of the "true" sense of words (what is the true sense of *etymon?*). But we must not be misled by such a proposition. Learned etymology is very, or not very different from so-called popular or literary etymologies—etymologies by affinity and no longer solely by filiation. It is a statistically probable science, dependent not only upon philological research that is never complete, but also upon the particular tropes of language that at certain periods come to dominate implicitly (today, it is metonymy and metaphor: everything revolves around these two figures—"irreplaceable porcelain dogs," Gérard Genette says, with pertinent irony). Why does filiation impress us so? The oldest sense of a word in the same or in different languages seems to restore or revive the meaning which ordinary language employs in a worn-out form or uses precisely because of its erosion. The supposition is that the oldest is the nearest to pure truth, or recalls what has been lost. This is an illusion, whether fertile or not. Jean Paulhan has shown that etymology cannot provide proof. Like Benveniste and in concert with him, Paulhan showed that we do not necessarily trace back etymologically to a more concrete, indeed a more "poetic" meaning, since numerous examples prove, or appear to prove, that "abstraction" precedes, just as unmotivatedness precedes motivation. To come back to the etymology of *alèthéia*, in which Heidegger, with admirable perseverance, sets such store: there is still no explanation why, though it reveals Greek thought, it seems to have been unknown to the Greeks—and why Plato (perhaps playfully, but what seriousness there is in this play) reads *alè-théia*, uncovering a meaning which could be translated as divine wandering and which is of no less importance than Heidegger's etymological interpretation. Truth (what is commonly called truth) would mean, according to Plato's etymology, errant course, the straying of the gods. From which it follows that it is the word "divine"—*théia*—which first resounds in *alèthéia*, and thus that the negative *a* does not have a privileged function, even if one doubts that so old a word as *apeiron* can possibly have kept from decomposing except by emphasizing the negation.

Still, when Heidegger recognizes in the language capable of the word *alèthéia*—etymologically of such decisive significance—the most telling of all languages, he conducts himself, though neither he nor Hegel was naive, as naively as Hegel, who was delighted by the German language, said to be speculative because it includes the word *Aufhebung*. For both Hegel and Heidegger, the one with the help of a hypothetical (a probable) etymology, the other by a verbal analysis, *created* these words, philosophically or poetically — these dawnlike words from which there arises a day of thought whose light for the time being none can escape. (Heidegger: "It is the most sublime dowry that the language of the Greeks received." And yet, according to Heidegger himself, the *alèthéia*, as it is thought of without being thought, does not yet belong to the Greek language, for there is no Greek language and no logos except through the *alèthéia*, which is preserved from every gaze upon truth and even upon being. However, it must be said as well that it "plays in the totality of the Greek language," and that if Heraclitus does not encounter it, does not expose himself to it, it is because of the predominance in him, and also thanks to him, of the *logos*: a blockage, as it were, of *a-lètheia* by *legein*. Finally, there is cause to remark that if *alètheia* is understood and translated into French as *désabritement* [a "de-sheltering"] — such is the translation momentarily chosen by Baufret and Janicaud — this is an altogether different movement of thought, an altogether different direction from the one which the most common translation — the "unveiled" [*le non-voilé*], the "unconcealed" [*le non-caché*], the "disclosure" [*le dévoilement*] — proposes. *Désabritement* is a possibility because of the reference to *bergen* in the German word *Unverborgenheit*. *Bergen*: to hide, safeguard, entrust to a protected place, to shelter [*abriter*]. *Alètheia* as *désabritement* leads back to wandering, to the meaning that Plato had suggested in the *Cratylus*. Whence the precaution of not overemphasizing the too-well-known phrase: "language, the house of being." Even in Plato, the myth of the cave is also the myth of the shelter: to forsake what shelters, to turn away, to unshelter oneself, is not only one of the major peripeties of knowledge; more importantly, it is the condition of a "veering round of the whole being," as Plato also says — a turning which puts us face to face with the demand of the turning point. That one or another way of translating should engage thought to this degree may be surprising; one might complain of this and conclude that philosophy is just a matter of words. There is no answer to that, except that one must always wonder, as Paulhan suggested, why a word is always more than a word. And Valéry: "The philosophical task still to be accomplished would consist in referring the *words* of philosophy's accomplishments back to history." But let us return to the most insistent question: is not the significance accorded to the fragile science of etymology excessive, which is to say, too facile?)

Regardless of its exactitude or imprecision, etymology fixes the attention upon the *word* as the seminal cell of language, and thus reverts to the ancient prejudice according to which language would be essentially made of names: a nomenclature. (Valéry said some time ago that one of the errors of philosophy is to limit itself to *words* and to neglect *sentences*: "O philosophers, what should be elucidated is not words . . . but sentences.") But this does not resolve anything either. The privilege accorded the verb, which reduces the noun to the status of an action that has simply been congealed, leads—even if it impedes the Cratylist option, and makes etymological creation more difficult—to the same, scarcely modified problems: sentences, series of sentences, sentences being born and fading away in one language or in a plurality of languages. As soon as we write, we carry these problems around with us, thinking without thinking about them. The least word, as Humboldt said, already presupposes the whole of language, the entire grammar of a language.

And finally, the learned delirium of etymology bears a relation to an historical vertigo. The entire history of a language opens up under the pressure of certain words and is by this genealogy either mystified or demystified. We think and speak dependent upon a past of which we demand an account, or which supports us, not without honor, in its forgottenness. The writer who plays with, or invents etymologies, or, more surreptitiously, appeals to etymology as a guarantee of his thought, is less dubious than exaggeratedly confident about the creative force of the language he speaks. He has in mind the vitality of language, popular inventiveness, or the intimacy of a dialect: always he thinks of language as a dwelling; always it is habitable language—language, our shelter. And right away we feel rooted, and so we pull at this root with an uprooting force which the demand of writing wields, just as it tends to tear us from everything natural—for the etymological series reconstitutes the becoming of language as a kind of historical *nature*.

The other danger of etymology is not simply its implicit relation to an origin, and the marvelously improbable resources that it seductively uncovers. Rather, the danger is that etymology imposes, without being able to justify or even to explain it, a certain conception of history. This conception is far from clear: the necessity of some provenance, of successive continuity, the logic of homogeneity, the revelation of sheer chance as destiny and of words as the sacred depository of all lost or latent meanings whose recovery is thenceforth the task of him who writes in view of a last word or final rebuttal (fulfillment, realization). Etymology and eschatology seem thus to be complicitous, and beginning and end to presuppose each other, the better to arrive at the presence of all presences, or parousia. But the seriousness of etymology, which has already abandoned scientific seriousness, has for an analogue, or for compensation, etymological fantasies, those farces which have always run wild at certain moments and which, as soon as the science of language has imposed practically certain gains, no longer appear as anything but follies: a language revery, the play of desire destined to free itself from knowledge even while exhibiting the lexical mirage, or to mime, simply for fun, the usage of the unconscious. At length, no one enjoys or finds any distraction in this, which is also of no importance. Except that skepticism appears to make some gains; but skepticism demands more.

◆ What is the justification of the relation that Heidegger establishes between *Ereignis,* whose ordinary meaning is "event," *Eraügnis,* to which he likens *Ereignis* (in a move sanctioned by the famous German dictionary *Duden; Eraügnis* is an archaic word in which one can glimpse the word "eye," *Auge:* thus, *Eraügnis* appeals to the gaze and suggests that being looks to us; once again being and light are linked), and finally *Ereignis* with its syllables divided in such a way that the word *eigen,* "proper," stands our, and the "event" becomes that which causes "the most proper" to befall out being? (*Duden* disqualifies the etymological relation between *eigen,* "proper," and *Ereignis.*) It is not the arbitrariness that is surprising here, but on the contrary, the mimetic effort, the semblance of analogy, the appeal to a doubtful body of knowledge that makes us the dupes of a kind of transhistorical necessity. It is true that the demand for a "justification" can, in its turn, here as elsewhere, be heard and then rejected. For there is nothing to justify; it is not a matter of right or wrong; rather, we are summoned to think and to question. Heidegger said: "Never *believe* anything; everything requires testing." That is why we too are questioning, recognizing in this test a process which is philologically and philosophically onerous.

♦ Let us grant that the word *eigen,* as it is mysteriously contained by *Ereignis,* does not mean anything at all like "property" or "appropriation"; let us acknowledge that *eigen* is boundless, inasmuch as "being" is no longer commensurate with it and cannot be determined therein. But why *eigen,* why "proper" (how else can this word be translated?), and not "improper"? Why this word? Why "presence" in its stubborn (patient) affirmation, which makes us repudiate "absence"? Earlier, in *Sein und Zeit,* the opposition between "authenticity" and "inauthenticity" (a superficial translation) prefigured—in a way that was still traditional—the more enigmatic question of the "proper," which ultimately we cannot welcome in the same way we do the undecidedness in "a-propriation" (Derrida). The "proper" cannot be welcomed in the lack of a place and of truth. Yet without this void, the gift of writing, the gift of sheer Saying— giving life as well as death, and being as well as not-being—would no longer be the expenditure which dislocates every event. "Improper" or "a-propriation," inasmuch as the "proper" is admitted in these expressions which at the same time disqualify it, calls to what obligates us limitlessly and cannot possibly be authorized by any truth, not even by one understood as nontruth. Thus does straying stray along its own path. (Let us not forget that for Heidegger, among the traits that characterize the *Ereignis* is its retreat, designated by *Enteignen-Enteignis* — or de-propriation.)

◆ Neither reading nor writing, nor speaking — and yet it is by those paths that we escape what has been said already, and knowledge, and reciprocity, and enter the unknown space, the space of distress where what is given is perhaps not received by anyone. Generosity of the disaster. There death, and life are always surpassed.

◆ The gift of writing is precisely what writing refuses. He who no longer knows how to write, who renounces the gift which he has received, whose language is unrecognizable, is closer to the untried inexperience, closer to the absence of the "proper" which, even without being, gives place to the advent. Whoever praises style, the originality of style, only exalts the self of the writer who has refused to abandon everything and to be abandoned by everything. Soon, he will be famous; notoriety hands him over to power: then what he lacks is effacement, disappearance.

Neither reading, nor writing, nor speaking: this is not muteness, but perhaps a murmur utterly unheard of: thunder and silence.

◆ *"Only he who one day has abandoned everything and has been abandoned by everything, for whom everything has capsized and who sees himself alone with the infinite, has come to the very bottom of himself and recognized all the profundity of life. This is a great step which Plato compared to death."* (Schelling, cited by Heidegger.)

◆ Why yet another book, where a seismic shuddering — one of the forms of the disaster — lays waste to it? Because the order of the book is required by what the book does not contain — by the absence which eludes the book. Likewise, the "proper" of "appropriation" — the event to which man and being both belong — plummets into the improperness of writing which escapes the law—escapes the mere vestige, as well as the rule, of secure meaning. But the improper is not simply the negation of the "proper"; it turns away from, by turning toward, the "proper." It makes "properness" unfathomable, for it maintains by dissolving this illusion. Proper still resounds in the improper: as the absence of a book, that which is exterior to any book makes what it surpasses heard. Whence the appeal to the fragmentary and the recourse to the disaster, if we remember that the disaster is not only the disastrous.

◆ Why still more books, if not in order to experience their tranquil, their tumultuous end which only the "effort" of writing brings about, when the dispersion of the subject—the proliferation of the multiple—delivers us to that "task of death" which M'Uzan speaks of. But this "task" cannot be limited, as he would have it, to the job of exhausting life—causing life, through the constant renewal of desire, to be lived completely. I recognize in this task rather the passion, the patience, the extreme passivity which opens life to dying and which is uneventful in the way that the already crossed out "biography"—a life of writing and a dying of writing (biography in the sense that Roger Laporte proposes that solitary name to us)—allows nothing to happen, and guarantees nothing, not even the act of writing. All of this restores to the secretness of the neutral that shade, to whom you assign the secure, quasi-professional appellation: writer.

◆ He wrote, whether this was possible or not, but he did not speak. Such is the silence of writing.

◆ "To write is incessant, and yet the text only advances by leaving behind lacunae, gaps, tears, and other interruptions, but the breaks themselves are rapidly reinscribed, at least so long as . . . " (Roger Laporte). —"To write . . . could constitute much more than a new genre." But "if to Write demands and yet disqualifies all writing, all typography, every book, then how can anyone write?" . . . "I no longer understand how I can for so long have identified with the esthetic project of creating a new genre." "To write has been crossed out only with an oblique mark. I must complete the work of destruction." (R. L.)

◆ " . . . to save a text from its book misfortune." (Levinas.)

◆ What has happened has not happened: thus spoke patience, that the end might not be hurried.

◆ "I" die before being born.

◆ Materialism: "my own" would perhaps be of little account, since it is appropriation or egotism; but the materialism of others — their hunger, their thirst, their desire — is the truth of materialism, its importance.

◆ There is an active, productive way of reading which produces text and reader and thus transports us. Then there is a passive kind of reading which betrays the text while appearing to submit to it, by giving the illusion that the text exists objectively, fully, sovereignly: as one whole. Finally, there is the reading that is no longer passive, but is passivity's reading. It is without pleasure, without joy; it escapes both comprehension and desire. It is like the nocturnal vigil, that "inspiring" insomnia when, all having been said, "Saying" is heard, and the testimony of the last witness pronounced.

◆ Last witness, end of history, close of a period, turning point, crisis — or, end of (metaphysical) philosophy.
  Even in Heidegger, in the course of a seminar whose orientation he seems to have sanctioned by his presence, the question of entry into the advent (*Ereignis,* with all the associations this word evokes) leads to discussion of the end of the history of being, in these cautious terms: "There is reason to meditate upon whether being, and thus the history of being, can still be spoken of after the entry into the advent; this is the case, at least, if the history of being is understood as the history of the endowments, the gifts in which the

advent *(Ereignis)* keeps withdrawn." But it is doubtful whether
Heidegger would recognize his own thinking in such a proposition,
whose merit is its temerity and whose meaning is only too clear: the
donations which are the ways in which being gives by withholding
itself (*logos* in Heraclitus, *One* in Parmenides, *Idea* in Plato, *energéia*
in Aristotle if we stay with the Greeks, and the final, modern version, *Gestell*—for which Lacoue-Labarthe proposes this equivalent:
"installation") would be interrupted from the moment that the
Ereignis, the advent, arrives, ceasing to let itself be hidden by the
"donations of meaning" which it makes possible by its retreat. But
if (since there is no other way of putting this) a decisive historical
change is announced in the phrase "the coming comes," making us
come into our "most proper," our "own-most" (being), then one
would have to be very naive not to think that the requirement to
withdraw ceases from then on. And yet it is from then one that
"withdraw" rules—more obscurely, more insistently. For what of
eigen, our "own-most" being? We do not know, except that it refers
back to *Ereignis,* just as *Ereignis* "hides" *eigen* all the while showing it
in a necessarily crude verbal analysis. Once again, nothing is said
when all is said by the most prudent of thinkers: nothing, except
that the question of the end of the history of being arises—with
Heidegger, who does not raise it directly. Similarly, Hegel leaves to
others the abrupt formulation "end of history."

Why does writing—when we understand this movement as the
change from one era to a different one, and when we think of it as
the experience (the inexperience) of the disaster—always imply the
words inscribed at the beginning of this "fragment," which, however, it revokes? It revokes them even if what they announce is announced as something new which has always already taken place, a
radical change from which the present tense is excluded.

As for the affirmation of history—realm of a dialectic other than
Hegelian, a so-called infinite dialectic of the here-and-now—as for
the idea of a history without either progress or regress (not circular):
it is no more able than any other concept or affirmation to escape the

multiple demands whose pressure is inscribed in the form of an *era*. To write in ignorance of the philosophical horizon—or refusing to acknowledge the punctuation, the groupings and separations determined by the words that mark this horizon—is necessarily to write with facile complacency (the literature of elegance and good taste). Hölderlin, Mallarmé, so many others, do not permit this.

◆ The postulates of etymology: the infinite is constituted with respect to the finite, as its negation-insertion (the infinite is the non-finite and is also *in* the finite); likewise *alèthéia* is assumed to have its meaning with respect to, and within, *lèthé*. But we can always refuse this lexical analysis. We can always posit and half perceive that the demand of the infinite, either as a vague sentiment or as the *a priori* of all comprehension, or again as a whole (a supertotality) always in the act of surpassing, is necessary in order that we know the word "finite" and grasp the idea of finitude (Descartes). In other words, the infiniteness of language as an infinite whole is always presupposed in order that the delimitation of a single word—and of the word "finite"— might intervene.

The Greek experience, as we reconstitute it, accords special value to the "limit" and reemphasizes the long-recognized scandalousness of the irrational: the indecency of that which, in measurement, is immeasurable. (He who first discovered the incommensurability of the diagonal of the square perished; he drowned in a shipwreck, for he had met with a strange and utterly foreign death, the nonplace bounded by absent frontiers; cf. Desanti.) The reference, which Hegel introduced, to a good and an evil infinite is suggestive: the qualifiers "good" and "evil" alone are provocative. The bad infinite—the "and so on" of the finite—is the infinite which the understanding (and the understanding is by no means bad) depends upon, as it freezes, fixes, immobilizes one of its moments. The truth of reason, on the other hand, suppresses the finite. The infinite—or the finite suppressed (suppressed *and* "conserved")—is "positive" in the sense that it reintroduces the qualitative and reconciles quality and quantum. What of the bad infinite, then? Abandoned to repetition without return, does it not affront the Hegelian system like a disaster? This is the same as suggesting that if the infinite can be defined as that which is given first, and which gives place, then, to the finite, this immediate infinite would disarrange the entire system, but only in the way that Hegel has always accounted for in advance, with ironic remarks about the nocturnal infinite. Finally, the appeal to a "present, given infinite" cannot be derived, even naively, from Cantor's transfinite.

Nonetheless we are insidiously (inevitably) subject to etymological clues which we take for proofs and from which we draw philosophical conclusions that secretly influence us. Such is the danger, indeed the abuse which brings into doubt much more than the recourse to etymology.

♦ Was the Greeks' understanding of *alètheia* based upon the meaning of *lèthē*? This is doubtful. And that we should be able to substitute ourselves for them — saying that they were nonetheless determined by this unthought element in their understanding — is a philosophical move to which there would be no objection, if it were not that we make it by wielding a philological expertise, thus making philosophy dependent upon a particular discipline. This contradicts the relations clearly affirmed by Heidegger between thought and determined bodies of knowledge. All such fields require a "foundation" which they cannot provide, and which thought is destined to give to each one by withdrawing it from each (except for mathematics, say some mathematical philosophers).

♦ *Ereignis*, thought's "final" word, does not, perhaps, put into play anything but the play of the idiom of desire.

♦ Nietzsche: *"As if my survival were something necessary."* Nietzsche means personal religious immortality; and he doubts that it is right or important to desire eternity. One should go further than that: even the desire of one's own ephemeralness — in the instant never over, or in the instant that vanishes right away—is still too much. Life without any of the surpassing indicated by the prefix of "survival"—life in the absence of any relation of temporal necessity, life which is without any present and which universal duration (the concept of time) does not govern, any more than the intimate singularity of a lived time affirms it—this is what best exposes time: pure difference, the *lapse* of time, the unbridgeable interval which, crossed, becomes limitless by virtue of the impossibility of any crossing (it is impossible to cross, inasmuch as always it is already crossed). The transcendence that living is, and that cannot be satisfactorily expressed in life itself as sur-vival (a surpassing of life), is rather the pressing demand of an *other* life, the life of the other. From this life everything comes, and turned to it, we cannot turn back. "As if survival (super-life) [*la survie (sur-vie)*] were necessary to life": the quick of living, the liveliness of this mortal hurt—life's retreat at the same time as its donation—disqualify the simple transcendence of projects undertaken, and the present soon to come which projects aim for, and the intentionality of a consciousness. Instead of finality, the burn of life which cannot burn out. From this fever all ending is excluded, all coming to a finish in a presence. Infinite, as unforeseen, foreboding. Forgetfulness, remembrance of the immemorial, without recollection.

♦ "That forgetfulness exists: this remains to be proved." (Nietzsche.) Exactly: unproven, improbable forgetfulness, vigilance that ever reawakens us.

♦ Nietzsche against the Superman: *"We are definitely ephemeral." "Humanity cannot accede to a superior order."* Let us consider *"the funeral urn of the last man."* This refusal of a man beyond man (in *Dawn*), is linked to everything Nietzsche said in warning against the peril of entrusting oneself to drunkenness and ecstacy as if this were the true life in life. Likewise, his disgust for *"the passionate but misguided, ecstatic men who pursue instants of ravishment from which they fall into the misery of vengefulness."* Intoxication has the weakness of giving us a feeling of strength.

♦ The healthy mistrust of language which Neitzsche teaches us usually—despite his ambiguous denunciation of "grammar"—concerns the excessive, uncontrolled importance granted to isolated words: "Wherever men placed a word, they believed they had made a discovery. . . . They had grazed a problem." But is that not already quite a bit? When he berates "petrified, eternalized words," it is because he wants to come back to language as dialectic or to a tearing, a disordering and ex-terminating movement which operates in language and which Humboldt had already vaguely evoked when he spoke of the spiritual dynamism of language, its infinite mediation. Today, linguists would have no difficulty in answering Nietzsche. And yet the suspicion, while it has changed form, has not been laid to rest.

Another complaint of Nietzsche's, formulated in a surprising manner: "It might be said that we have words only for *extremes* of feeling"—joy, pain—and that we miss the greyish, scarcely felt underside of life which is its becoming. But the opposite may be the case: that we have no words for the extreme; that dazzling joy and great pain burn up every term and render them all mute. (An etymological paradox: if *éblouissement* ["bedazzlement"] is linked to the German *blöde,* whose meaning is first "weak" and then "weaksighted," it is surprising that an excess of light, which blinds, should be expressed in terms of a kind of myopia, a deficiency of the eye. What attracts us to etymology is its unreasonable part more than what it explains: we are interested by the form of enigma that it preserves or doubles as it deciphers). But is Nietzsche not simply noticing, as Bergson would later, that words are suitable only for the crude analysis of abstract understanding ("extreme," then, would mean: what is unmistakable, schematic)? Here again, suspicion is not suspicious enough.

♦ Valéry: *"The thinker is locked in a cage and paces indefinitely between four words.*" What is said pejoratively here is not pejorative: repetitive patience, infinite perseverance. And the same Valéry — is it the same one? — will come to affirm in passing: *"To think? . . . To think! It is to lose the thread."* A hasty commentary: surprise, the interval, discontinuity.

◆ Roots, an invention of grammarians (Bopp) (in other words, a theoretical fiction — but language theory is no more fictive than any other field of study). Or, Schlegel says, *"just as the name tells us,"* "a living germ always at work in language." *Just as the name tells us* (the name, here, being "root"): this appeal to the name shows the circular reasoning — the circularity from which all languages draw their fecundity: the root having been named by analogy with plant growth and with the supposed unity of a germinating principle hidden beneath the earth, we draw from there the idea that the root is the formative germ by which words, in diverse languages, receive the power of development, and creative enrichment. Once again, believers and nonbelievers are both wrong and right. A writer who, like Heidegger, goes back to the root of certain words which are said to be fundamental, and receives from this root an impulse to develop variations upon certain thoughts and words, makes the idea that there is in the root a strength that works and that incites to work, "true."

◆ That even Humboldt, who is usually so prudent, should go from internal analogy — a relation inside language ("autosignification") — to external analogy — imitation of the world, of things, of being in general (the real) by words through their *sonority,* which he had already disqualified when he distinguished the moment of articulation from the sheer sound of the voice — shows how irresistible is the temptation to "denature" the process of signification by naturalizing it. (Contrary to what contemporary commentators held, Humboldt saw in the following sequence of verbal similitudes — *wehen* ["to breathe"], *Wind* ["wind"], *Wolke* ["cloud"], *wirren* ["to trouble"], *Wunsch* ["wish"] — the reflection of "fluctuations, turbu-

lences, vacillations received by the senses—sensory impressions—
which are *rendered* by the *W*, a contraction of the mute *U*.") It is true
that Humboldt modifies this idea of imitation and does not give it
any decisive importance. More significant is the "transcendence" of
language in and of itself: that is to say, a given language enters into
resonance with itself and determines itself without end; it constitutes, thus, an interrupted, uninterrupted action, which then causes
"the soul to enter into resonance with itself or with the object." "A
particular language can be compared to an immense fabric in which
each part is entwined with all the others and where all belong to the
whole according to a more or less perceptible cohesion." Humboldt
will call this cohesion the underlying whole of the system. (When
Humboldt writes: "That there is a close connection between the
phonetic element and its meaning is incontestable, but it is only
rarely that one can systematically apprehend the organization of this
relation: most often one can have only a diffuse impression of it, and
its deep nature escapes us," he is simply hesitating, and still expressing himself cautiously. Finally, Humboldt uses the word "symbol"
similarly to the way Hegel does: the symbol makes the unrepresentable speakable, showable: "The symbol has the power to invite and
to cause the mind to abide near the representation" of that which
cannot be represented—the pure transcendent. Elsewhere, Humboldt speaks of "the irreducible difference between the concept and
the phonetic element.")

♦ Whatever Gérard Genette may say to the contrary (perhaps) of
what he himself thinks, Hermogenes' ascetic refusal is not sterile,
because we owe to this austerity the possibility of the field of linguistics, and because no writer ever writes unless he bears Hermogenes in mind in order to reject (even if, eventually, he does yield
to them) all facile mimetic tricks and in order to arrive at a completely different practice.

♦ Why is the necessity of the gift so regularly expressed in our
time, and yet assigned such different significance by thinkers as

adverse and diverse as Georges Bataille, Emmanuel Levinas, Heidegger? This question is worth asking even if there is no fitting or coherent answer. To evoke Nietzsche and Mauss for Bataille only enables us to pick out certain fixed terms, crystallizations of problems which had already long been pressing in his thought. The movement toward the other—the movement Bataille calls heterology—precedes, in his work, what the words "gift" or "expenditure" are meant to designate: the subversion of order, transgression, restitution of a more general economy which would not be dominated by the administration of objects (utility). But impossible loss—linked to the idea of sacrifice and to the experience of sovereign instants—does not allow the tensions which rip thought apart, and which the harshness of a restless language maintains, to congeal into a system. The similarity with Levinas—perhaps deceptive, perhaps superficial (for the philosophical horizon is different)—comes from the same word "other"which, in Levinas, means the transcendence of another person: the infinite relation of one person to another obligates beyond any obligation. This leads to the idea of the gift, not as the gracious act of a free subject, but as detachment, a disinterestedness which is *suffered* and whereby, beyond all activity and all passivity, patient responsibility endures all the way to "substitution," "one for the other." Thus is the infinite given without being able to be exchanged.

Where Heidegger is concerned, we must not stop at quick interpretations of what he has been understood to think (or of translations of his thought). "The history of being is considered as the history of the *donations* in which the advent *(Ereignis)* holds itself in abeyance"; whence the simple-minded question: "Would entrance into the advent mean the end of the history of being?" The word "donation" is *given* by the German expression for "there is" [in French, *il y a*]: *Es gibt:* "it gives." "It," the impersonal third person, is the "subject" of the *Ereignis*—of the coming of the most proper. If we are content to say, "Being gives itself whereas time withdraws," then we say nothing, for we understand "Being" as though it were a determined being that gives, gives itself and favors. Whereas Heidegger says firmly: "Presence (being) belongs to the clearing—the clearness—of withdrawal (time). Clearing of withdrawal (time) brings presence (being) with it." Without drawing any conclusions from this, we receive the donation in its constant relation with presence (being). "The coming comes" (presence of all presences, parousia)—likewise "the word speaks"—is the gift of the word in that it pronounces the multiple richness of the *Same* which never is identical.

What Bataille and Levinas have in common, or what is similar in one and in the other, is the gift as the inexhaustible (the infinite) demand of the other and of others, a demand that calls for nothing less than impossible loss: the gift of interiority. In Heidegger the retention of the Same and the experience of presence is different. But the "is given," or the "it gives," can never, regardless of the precisions introduced by "the advent," have any explicit subject. Who gives? What is given? These are questions which no formulation suits, and which resound in language without receiving any answer other than language itself, the gift of language.

Whence the dangerous leaning toward the sanctification of language. The spontaneous tendency of romanticism is to link the recognition of the religious character of all language to ancient, primordial times. A.W. von Schlegel: "The word was first a cult, then the study of language became a profession." "Language, the house of being." But let us repeat with Levinas, even though he accords special value to Speaking as the gift of significance: "Language is in itself already skepticism." To write is to be absolutely distrustful of writing, while entrusting oneself to it entirely. Whatever basis one may assign to this double movement—which is not as contradictory as its excessively concise formulation makes it seem—it is still the rule of every writing practice: "giving withholding" has, in writing's double imperative, I won't say its application, or its illustration, for these are scarcely adequate terms, but—through the dialectic and also without regard to it at all—that which justifies itself simply by letting itself be said right from the moment that there is saying — and by virtue of which there is saying.

◆ Let us not be too tempted by the affirmations of knowledge such as Leroi-Gourhan commands when he describes the first evidence of writing as a series of "small notches" arranged at regular intervals. Still, let us not fail to welcome this thought. It suggests that in this pattern, the energy of repetition — in other words, rhythm — is at work. Design and inscription, art and writing, not distinct from each other. One more affirmation: "If there is a point about which we can now be certain, it is that written signs begin, not as naive representations, but as abstractions." Let us make no objection, but simply bear in mind that "abstraction" means abstract *for us,* which is to say, from our point of view, separation, a setting apart. Thus we come back to the great verdict which it is always right and necessary to contest, on the condition that one not cease to think it unthinkable. Todorov: "Diachronically, one could not conceive of the origin of language without positing first off the absence of objects." And Leroi-Gourhan: "This amounts to making language the instrument of liberation with respect to lived reality." Reserving any conclusion with regard to these somewhat hasty formulations, one can say: such is the requirement, in language, of the process of *signification.* It does not just disqualify the "object," "the lived"; it excludes the very significance of signification, in an extreme movement which ultimately escapes, while remaining nonetheless in operation. But language also contains the *symbol*, where the symbolizer and the symbolized can be part of one another (this is said in a vocabulary which is only ever approximate), where the unrepresentable is *present* in the representation which it exceeds, or in any case linked thereto by a certain "motivated" relation introduced by culture (it will immediately be thought: natural), reinstating between sign and "thing" an unstable presence-absence which art — and art as literature — maintains and regenerates. (Cf. Todorov's remarks in *Poétique* 21.)

◆ An example of etymological fictions: "Rhythm": the staid and probably "erroneous" etymology refers us to *sreu* and *rheô*, "to flow"; whence *rhuthmos*, the welling up and sinking back of what flows (and rhythms and rhymes). [19] But no one will then state whether it is some regular beat always already in operation that made it possible to recognize the coming and going of the waves, or the special experience of the seascape that independently conveyed the feeling—which otherwise would have gone unnoticed—of repetition. The great number of repetitive phenomena (breathing in and out, *fort-da*, day-night, etc.) make this latter hypothesis rather doubtful. Here again, traditional etymology gives the illusion of a "concrete" example, of an exemplary phenomenon (and of a body of sure knowledge). We evoke men of the sea, brave navigators, frightened and also enchanted, mastering the most dangerous unknown (that marine infinitude which both buoys and engulfs), by observing a regular movement, a first legality. Everything comes from the sea for men of the sea, just as everything comes from the sky for others, who recognize a given cluster of stars and who designate, in the magic "configuration" of those points of light, the nascent rhythm which already governs their entire language and which they speak (write) before naming it.

◆ Let us recall Hölderlin: "All is rhythm," he is supposed to have said to Bettina—according to a report, Sinclair's, which she may have imagined. How is this sentence to be understood? "All" does not mean the cosmic in an already ordered totality which it would be rhythm's job to maintain. Rhythm does not belong to the order of nature or of language, or even of "art," where it seems to predominate. Rhythm is not the simple alternation of Yes and No, of "giving-withholding," of presence-absence or of living-dying, producing-destroying. Rhythm, while it disengages the multiple from its missing unity, and while it appears regular and seems to govern according to a rule, threatens the rule. For always it exceeds the rule through a reversal whereby, being in play or in operation within measure, it is not measured thereby. The enigma of rhythm—dialectical-nondialectical, no more the one than the other is other—is the extreme danger. That we should speak in order to make sense of rhythm, and to make rhythm—which is not sensible—perceptible and meaningful: such is the mystery which traverses us; we will not free ourselves from it by revering it as sacred.

◆ *"Optimists write badly."* (Valéry.) But pessimists do not write.

◆ The shortcut does not allow one to arrive someplace more directly (more quickly), but rather to lose the way that ought to lead there.

◆ To question ourselves too openly about rhythm is to relate rhythm and the open and, in a way, to open ourselves to rhythm only by submitting to it obsessively, letting it become the sole Subject to open the open, the Subject that marks the open rhythmically the way certain official clauses repetitively mark contracts. Rhythm is no Subject, unless it be abused. "All is rhythm" does not mean—this would be too little and too much—rhythm is the totality of all. But no more does it mean that rhythm is just a mode, as though we were to say: all that is, is rhythmically. We must, however, try to reach such an affirmation. For that relation of being to rhythm—that inevitable relation—would enable us not to think of being without thinking of rhythm, which is, but is not commensurate with being. This is another way of letting oneself be questioned by difference.

◆ Melville–René Char: *"The infinite desiring suddenly recedes."* (Char.) Melville suggests a violent shock: the ardent, infinite attraction is the fright that repels. The absolute desiring (the infinite which in relation with desire would be the infinitude of desire) not only goes by way of "without desire," but demands fright, measureless retreat through measureless attraction.

◆ We do not repel the earth, to which, in any event, we belong; but we do not make of it a refuge, or even of dwelling upon it a beautiful obligation, *"for terrible is the earth."* The disaster, always belated—the disaster, strangled sleep—could remind us of this, if there were memory of the immemorable.

◆ If *"in*discretion with respect to the *in*effable" (E.L.) is perhaps our task, then this task is stated by the relation between the same prefix repeated—"in"—and the ambiguity which this prefix gets from the infinite. The ineffable, the unspeakable would be circumscribed by Speaking raised to infinity. For what escapes all that can be said is not only what must be said; it escapes only under the auspices of Saying and when kept back by the restraint that is Saying's alone. Likewise, to be indiscreet is to fail, with the help of reserve, to be sufficiently reserved; it is to fail, by never, by always failing, to be reserved.

◆ "Radical change" might be conveyed if it were specified in the following manner: from what comes to pass, the present is excluded. Radical change would itself come in the mode of the un-present which it causes to come, without thereby either consigning itself to the future (foreseeable or not), or withdrawing into a past (transmitted or not).

◆ (A primal scene?) *"Indiscretion, ineffable, infinite, radical change: is there not, among what these words evoke, if not a relation, at least a necessary estrangement that would make them, by turns—or together—applicable to what has been termed a scene? —This term is ill-chosen, for what it supposedly names is unrepresentable, and escapes fiction as well; yet 'scene' is pertinent in that it allows one at least not to speak as if of an event taking place at a moment in time. —A scene: a shadow, a faint gleam, an 'almost' with the characteristics of 'too much,' of excessiveness, in sum. —The secret alluded to is that there is none, except for those who refuse to tell. —But it is unutterable inasmuch as narrated, proffered. —Not the Mallarméan 'proffer' (although it is impossible to avoid passing this way). I still remember: 'I proffer the word, in order to plunge it back into its nullity.' It is the 'in order,' the overly certain finality of nothingness, that lets us know we can-*

not stop and rest with Mallarmé's 'proffer.' We are thinking, rather, of something said which, without referring back to anything unspoken (as it has become customary to claim), or to an inexhaustible wealth of words, reserves sheer Saying which seems to denounce it, to authorize it, to provoke it to retract itself. —Saying: the power to say? This alters it immediately. Weakness would be more appropriate. —If propriety were not here improper. Then we might say: the gift of scantness, the gift of the poor, for lack of the loss never received. —But who recounts? —The story. —The pre-story, 'the flashing circumstance' whereby the dazzled child sees — he has the spectacle of it — the happy murder of himself which gives him words' silence. —The tears are also a child's. —Tears of a whole life, of all lives, the absolute dissolution which, be it joy or sorrow, the face, in its invisibility childish, lifts up, in order to shine in this dissolution and keep shining all the way to emotion that gives no sign at all. —Immediately banally interpreted. —Banality makes no mistake; it is consolation's commentary whereby solitude is shut out, refused all shelter. —Let me continue to emphasize the banality: the circumstances are of this world— the tree, the wall, the winter garden, the play space and with it, lassitude; then time is introduced, and its discourse: the recountable is either without any episode of note, or else purely episodic. Indeed, the sky, in the cosmic dimension it takes on as soon as it is named— the stars, the universe— brings only the clarity of parsimonious daylight, even if this were to be construed as the 'fiat lux.' —It is a distantness that is not distant. —Nevertheless, the same sky . . . —Exactly, it has to be the same. —Nothing has changed. —Except the overwhelming overturning of nothing. —Which breaks, by the smashing of a pane (behind which one rests assured of perfect, of protected, visibility), the finite-infinite space of the cosmos— ordinary order— the better to substitute the knowing vertigo of the deserted outside. Blackness and void, responding to the suddenness of the opening and giving themselves unalloyed, announce the revelation of the outside by absence, loss and the lack of any beyond. —But 'the beyond,' stopped from having anything to do with this scene at all by the verdict of that emptied word 'nothing'— which is itself nothing— is quite to the contrary called into the scene, and from the opening moment: as soon as the revelation, as well as the tension of nothing, of being and of there is intervene and provoke the interminable shuddering. —I concede: 'nothing is what there is' rules out its being said in a calm and simple negation (as though in its place the eternal translator wrote 'There is nothing'). —No negation, but heavy terms, like whole stanzas juxtaposed while remaining without any connection, each one closed in self-sufficiency (but not upon any meaningfulness)—each one immobile and mute, and all of them thus usurping the sentence their relation forms, a sentence whose intended significance we would be hard put to explain. —Hard put is an understatement: there passes through this sentence what it can contain only by bursting. —For my part, I hear the inevitability of there is, which being and nothing roll like a great wave, unfurling it and folding it back under, inscribing and effacing it, to the rhythm of the nameless rustling. —To hear the echolessness of the voice: a strange hearing. —The hearing of strangeness. But let us go no further. —Having already been too far, returning. —Coming back toward the initial summons which proposes the fictive supposition, the 'scene.' Without it, to speak of the child who has never spoken would be to insert into history, into experience, or reality, as an episode or a tableau, that which has ruined them (history, experience, reality), leaving them intact. —The generous effect of the disaster. —The ancientness of the face without a single line. —The trauma of poetry and of philosophy, indistinct one from the other."

"The ever-suspended question: having died of this 'ability to die' which gives him joy and devastation, did he survive—or rather, what does to survive mean then, if not to be sustained by an assent to refusal, by the exhaustion of feeling, and to live withdrawn from any interest in oneself, disinterested, thinned out to a state of utter calmness, expecting nothing? —Consequently, waiting and watching, for suddenly wakened and, knowing this full well henceforth, never wakeful enough."

♦ Naturally, "disaster" can be understood according to its etymology—of which many fragments here bear the trace. But the etymology of "disaster" does not operate in these fragments as a preferred, or more original insight, ensuring mastery of what is no longer, then, anything but a word. On the contrary, the indeterminateness of what is written when this word is written, exceeds etymology and draws it into the disaster.

♦ That there is no awaiting the disaster is true to the extent that waiting is considered always to be the awaiting of something waited for, or else unexpected. But awaiting — just as it is not related to the future any more than to an accessible past — is also the awaiting of awaiting, which does not situate us in a present, for "I" have always already awaited what I will always wait for: the immemorable, the unknown which has no present, and which I can no more remember than I can know whether I am not forgetting the future — the future being my relation with what, in what is coming, does not come and thus does not present, or re-present itself. That is why it is permitted, by the movement of writing, to say: You are already dead. And what is forgetfulness? It is not related to ignorance of the eventual present (the future), any more than it is loss of the memorable from the memory. Forgetfulness designates what is beyond possibility, the unforgettable Other; it indicates that which, past or future, it does not circumscribe: patience in its passive mode.

♦ There is no origin, if origin presupposes an original presence. Always past, long since past already, something that has passed without being present — such is the immemorial which gives us forgetfulness saying: every beginning is a beginning over.

♦ There is no doubt but that we weaken Heidegger's thought when we interpret "being-for-death" as the search for authenticity through death. We attribute to him the vision of a persevering humanism. To begin with, the term "authenticity" does not do justice to *Eigentlichkeit,* which already suggests the ambiguities of the word *eigen* as they are to appear in *Ereignis* — the "event" which cannot be understood in relation to "being." Nevertheless, even if we abandon the illusion of Rilke's "proper death," dying in this perspective still cannot be separated from the "personal"; still we neglect what is "impersonal" in death, with regard to which it must be said not that "I die," but that *somebody* dies, somebody who is no one in particular, who in dying is always other.

♦ Schelling: "The soul is the true, the impersonal divinity in man. . . . The soul is the nonpersonal." Or again: "To the extent that the human mind is related to the soul as to something nonexistent — something, that is, without understanding — its profoundest essence (in that it is separated from the soul and from God) is *madness*. The understanding is *regulated madness*. Men who have no madness in them are men whose understanding is void and sterile. . . ."

♦ If it is true that for a certain Freud, "our unconscious cannot conceive of our own mortality" (is unable to represent mortality to itself), then it would seem to follow that dying is unrepresentable, not only because it has no present, but also because it has no place, not even in time, the temporality of time. Likewise, if we must certainly reflect upon Pontalis' interpretation — (the unconscious) "knows nothing of negation because it *is* the negative, as opposed to the supposedly full positivity of life" — we must also remember that the "negative" is sometimes operative (speaking with language and related thus to "being"), and sometimes inoperative: the nonoperation of sheer inertia — endurance without duration (which is to say: patience), a pre-inscription which ever effaces itself as a production of meaning without thereby becoming meaningless, and which is suffered "in us" only as the death of others. Not as death itself, but as a death that is always other, with which we do not communicate, but for which we bear the unbearable responsibility. No relation, then (in death), to violence and aggression. But what mimes death — the unrepresentable representation — is detachment: it is rupture, but through very writing; fragmentation (but without closure); "a process without any purpose except to complete itself (or rather, to incomplete itself), and which is marked by its repetitive character with the imprint of the obsessional" (Pontalis). I will add that none of the current public images of the death drive (the atomic threat, etc.) has anything to do with the unrepresentable aspect of the death drive. These symbols are at most related to the first (Hegelian) sense of the negative: destruction in view of possible construction. Nothing can be done with death that has always taken place already: it is the task of idleness, a nonrelation with a past (or future) utterly bereft of present. Thus the disaster would be beyond what we understand by death or abyss, or in any case by *my* death, since there is no more place for "me": in the disaster I disappear without dying (or die without disappearing).

◆ Mortal, immortal: does this reversal have any meaning?

◆ Reading in R.B. what he does not say, but suggests, I imagine that for Werther the passion of love is but a roundabout way of dying.[20] After reading *Werther,* people did not fall in love in greater numbers; they killed themselves. And Goethe unburdened himself upon Werther of the temptation to die. But not of the temptation to die of his passion: Goethe didn't write in order not to die. Rather he wrote through the movement of a death no longer his own. *"That can only end badly."*

◆ The I that is responsible for others, the I bereft of selfhood, is sheer fragility, through and through on trial. This I without any identity is responsible for him to whom he can give no response; this I must answer in an interrogation where no question is put; he is a question directed to others from whom no answer can be expected either. The Other does not answer.

◆ I remain persuaded that the zeal of etymology is linked to a certain naturalism — that it is a kind of quest for an original secret held by a first, lost language, clues of which would subsist among the multiple tongues that now exist, permitting its reconstruction. This handily justifies the writing imperative, making it seem that through writing man possesses a personal secret which he could disclose innocently, without any other's knowing. But if there is a secret, it is in the infinite relation of the one to the other which the drift of meaning hides, because in it the one seems to preserve his necessity even in death.

But it is true that the idea of arbitrariness in linguistics is just as debatable, and that its value is above all ascetic: it heads us off from facile solutions. (Perhaps the idea of the arbitrariness of the sign already presupposes the implicit, concealed image of a "world.")

◆ The disaster—experience none can undergo—obliterates (while leaving perfectly intact) our relation to the world as presence or as absence; it does not thereby free us, however, from this obsession with which it burdens us: others. For the lack of reciprocity with the Other toward which it turns us—the immediate and infinite question—is no part of sidereal space, to which, were disaster the substitution of a radical heterogeneity, it would be subordinated. This does not mean that we are unconcerned for those who, unlike ourselves, suffer from an unjust order, our own suffering being ever justified—beyond justice. For we are responsible for whoever would cause us to suffer (we are responsible for others). It is not that we have to assume whatever evil they would cause us to suffer, but rather that the patience which surpasses every conceivable passive mode—the patience to which they assign us—leads us back toward a past without any present. The pseudo-intransitiveness of writing is linked to this patience which no complement—life or death—can ever complete.

◆ Naturally, the question already raised arises anew: if the obsession with others persists till it becomes a kind of persecution, and living becomes for us a way of dying, is this not the proof of a sort of cruelty on our part toward the other—that we should make him thus so cruel? But this is to forget that it is not up to me to welcome, or to bear whatever may be visited upon us. Through the passivity of patience, the self has nothing to undergo, for it has completely lost all the capacity of a privileged self, without ceasing to be responsible. There is no name anymore for such a "self," but this namelessness is not the crude anonymity defined by Kierkegaard:

"anonymity—supreme expression of abstraction, of impersonality, of unscrupulousness and irresponsibility—one of the profound sources of modern corruption." There are many confusions in this sentence, which seems to assume that anonymity is by definition the anonymity that operates in the world: for example, what is called bureaucratic anonymity.

♦ The writer, daytime insomniac.

♦ Granted, to write is to renounce being in command of oneself or having any proper name, and at the same time it is not to renounce, but to announce, welcoming without recognition the absent. Or, it is to be in relation, through words in their absence, with what one cannot remember—a witness to the unencountered, answerable not only for the void in the subject, but for the subject as a void, its disappearance in the imminence of a death which has already taken place, out of place, any place at all.

♦ Loss goes with writing. But a loss without any gift (a gift, that is, without reciprocation) is always liable to be a tranquilizing loss bringing security. That is why there is probably no amorous discourse, if not the language of love in its absence, "lived" in loss, in decline—that is, in death.

♦ If death is the real, and if the real is impossible, then we are approaching the thought of the impossibility of death.

♦ According to the disciple of Barl-Shem, the Rabbi Pinhas, we should love the wicked and hateful "more," in order to compensate with our love for the lack of love they have caused, and to mend this "rip" in the power of Love. But what do wickedness and hate mean? They are not traits of the Other, who is precisely the deprived, the abandoned, the destitute. If one can speak of hate and wickedness at all, it is because on account of them evil touches others, and thus justice demands their rejection, and that there be resistance, and even violence aimed at repelling violence.

♦ I should like to limit myself to a single word, kept pure and alive in its absence, if it weren't that through that one word, I have all the infiniteness of all languages to bear.

♦ "The least hint of anti-semitism manifested by a group or by an individual reveals the reactionary nature of this group or individual" (Lenin, quoted by Guillemin).

♦ To keep still, *preserving* silence: that is what, all unknowing, we all want to do, writing.

♦ Job: *"I spoke once. . . . I will not repeat; I twice. . . . I will not add anything."* This is perhaps what is signified by the repetitiveness of writing: writing repeats the ultimate to which there is nothing to add.

♦ What does Nietzsche occasionally say about Jews? "From the small Jewish community comes the principle of *love*: that is to say, a more *passionate* soul whose ardor smoulders beneath humility and poverty. This was neither Greek nor Hindu nor even Germanic. The hymn to charity that Paul composed has nothing Christian about it; it is the Jewish surging of the eternal flame, which is semitic. . . ." —"Every society has a tendency to degrade its adversaries till they appear only as a *caricature*. . . . In the system of aristocratic, Roman values, the *Jew* was reduced to a caricature. . . . Plato becomes a caricature in my writing. . . ." — "To hide one's envy of the mercantile intelligence of Jews beneath moral formulae: *that* is antisemitic—vulgar, and grossly indecent." Nietzsche understands very well that Jews become merchants because no other activity is permitted them. Whence this obscure wish announcing a different future for Jews: "Give to *Jews* the courage of *new virtues,* when they have passed into new conditions of existence. This is what suits my own instinct, and in this respect I have not allowed myself to be waylaid by a poisonous opposition which now, precisely, is having its way." These comments are to be found among many highly suspicious remarks, when Nietzsche no longer sees in Christianity anything but an emancipated Judaism, or when without reflecting he borrows his language from the Christian commonplaces of the time. But when anti-semitism becomes systematized, and an organized movement, he rejects it with horror. Who is unaware of this? (That Nietzsche's thought is dangerous, is certainly true. He is the first to teach us this: if you begin to think, then you can hope for no rest.)

◆ Nietzsche: "In the Jewish 'Old Testament,' that book of God's justice, we encounter men, events, and utterances of such great vitality that neither Greek nor Hindu literature offers anything comparable. One is seized with fear and respect before these prodigious vestiges of what man once was, and one entertains sad reflections about ancient Asia and her advanced peninsula, Europe, which claims to incarnate vis-à-vis Asia 'the progress of man.' . . ." — "To have stuck onto the Old, this New Testament — this monument in every respect to a rococo taste — in order to join the two in a single book, the Bible, *the* Book par excellence: this is perhaps the greatest imprudence, the greatest 'sin against the spirit' that modern literature has on its conscience." What does Nietzsche mean here? He is speaking of style and taste, of literature, but his use of these words elevates what they convey. And I take note of this: he mocks Greek civilization no less than Christian. Elsewhere, Christianity is praised for having been able to maintain respect for the Bible, even if it did so by forbidding that the Bible be read: "The way in which respect for the Bible has been maintained on the whole up until our own time, constitutes perhaps the best example of the discipline and cultural refinement that Europe owes to Christianity: books of this profundity — receptacles of an *ultimate significance* (my emphasis) — need to be protected by a tyrannical exterior authority in order to be sure of that *duration* of several thousands of years which is necessary for exhausting their meaning and comprehending it fully." What is said here is a judgment upon our judgments of Nietzsche, without, it is true, helping us at all to approach Judaism. Likewise, in another book, but in practically the same terms: "The Old Testament is really something! Hats off to the Old Testament! Here I find great men, a heroic landscape and one of the rarest things in the world, the incomparable naiveté of the *robust heart*; and furthermore, I find a people."

♦ In search neither of the place, nor of the formula.

♦ *"There is no explosion except a book."* A book: a book among others, or a reference to the unique, the last and essential *Liber,* or, more exactly, the great Book which is always one among others, any book at all, already without importance or beyond important things. "Explosion," a book: this means that the book is not the laborious assemblage of a totality finally obtained, but has for its being the noisy, silent bursting which without the book would not take place (would not affirm itself). But it also means that since the book itself belongs to burst being — to being violently exceeded and thrust out of itself — the book gives no sign of itself save its own explosive violence, the force with which it expels itself, the thunderous refusal of the plausible: the outside in its becoming, which is that of bursting.

The dying of a book in all books calls; and this is the call which must be answered — not by solemnly reflecting upon the circumstances of the times, on the crisis announced therein or the upheaval being prepared. These are great things, they are small things even if they demand everything of us (as Hölderlin said, ready to throw his pen under the table in order to belong completely to the Revolution). Yet the answer does concern time, an *other* time, another mode of temporality which no longer lets us be tranquilly our own contemporaries. But the answer is necessarily silent, utterly unassuming, always already interrupted, deprived of all propriety and adequacy — tacit, in that it can only ever be the echo of a language of explosion. Perhaps I should cite this always startling signal, these enlivening words of a poet very close to me: *"Listen, lend your ear: even books set quite apart, far from the fray — beloved books, essential books — are agonizing now."* (René Char.)

◆ (A primal scene?) It is typical of narcissism, defined carelessly or subtly, that, like La Rochefoucauld's *amour-propre*, its effect is easily discernible in everything everywhere. It suffices to form the adjective from the noun: what is there that isn't narcissistic? All the positions of being are narcissistic, and of not-being. Even when being is totally renounced—denied to the point of becoming not-being—it does not cease (with the element of ambiguity which then obscures it) to be passively active. Thus the rigors of spiritual purification, even the absolute withdrawal into the void can be seen as narcissistic modes: relatively undemanding ways for a disappointed subject, or one uncertain of his identity, to affirm by annulling himself. This doubt cast upon selflessness is not to be ignored. We encounter in it the dizzying occidental tendency to link all values back up with the Same, and this tendency is all the more pronounced when it is a matter of an ill-constituted "same"—the self—an evanescent identity which is lost even as it is grasped (here we recognize a favorite theme for certain dialectical meditations).

Mythologists do not fail to indicate that Ovid—an intelligent, civilized poet, upon whose version of the myth the concept of narcissism is modeled (as though his narrative developments indeed contained psychoanalytical knowledge)—modifies the myth in order to expand it and make it more accessible. But the aspect of the myth which Ovid finally forgets is that Narcissus, bending over the spring, does not recognize himself in the fluid image that the water sends back to him. It is thus not himself, not his perhaps nonexistent "I" that he loves or—even in his mystification—desires. And if he does not recognize himself, it is because what he sees is an image, and because the similitude of an image is not likeness to anyone or anything: the image characteristically resembles nothing. Narcissus falls "in love" with the image because the image as such—because every image—is attractive: the image exerts the attraction of the void, and of death in its falsity. The teaching of the myth—which, like all myths, resembles a fable to some extent and is instructive—would be that one must not entrust oneself to the fascination of images which not only deceive (whence the facile commentaries of Plotinus), but render all love mad. For a distance is necessary if desire is to be born of not being immediately satisfied. This is what Ovid, in his subtle additions, has expressed by having Narcissus say (as if Narcissus could speak, speak "to himself," utter a soliloquy): "Possession dispossessed me."

What is mythical in this myth is death's practically unnamed presence — in the water, in the spring, in the flowery shimmering of a limpid enchantment which does not open onto the frightfully unfathomable underground, but reflects it dangerously (crazily) in the illusion of a surface proximity. Does Narcissus die? Scarcely: having turned into an image, he dissolves in the immobile dissolution of the imaginary, where he is washed away without knowing it, losing a life he does not have. For if there is one thing to be retained from the classical commentators, who are always quick to rationalize, it is that Narcissus never began to live. This child-god (the story of Narcissus, let us not forget, is a story of gods or demigods) — never tolerating the touch of another, never speaking — did not know of himself, for, according to the command he is supposed to have received, he was to keep always turned away from himself. Thus he is very similar to the marvelous child about whom Serge Leclaire has spoken to us — always already dead and nonetheless destined to a fragile, attenuated dying.

Yes, a fragile myth, a myth of fragility. In the oscillating, intermediary zone between a consciousness not yet formed and an unconsciousness that lets itself be seen and thereby turns vision into fascination, one of the versions of the imaginary offers its lesson: man — is it man? — can make himself in accordance with the image, but this means that he is still more apt to unmake himself in accordance with the image, exposing himself to the illusion of a similitude which may be beautiful, or fatal, but which is in any case the illusion of an evasive death that consists entirely in the repetition of a mute misapprehension. Of course, the myth does not say anything so explicit. The Greek myths do not, generally, say anything; they are seductive because of a concealed, oracular wisdom which elicits the infinite process of divining. What we call meaning, or indeed sign, is foreign to them: they signal without signifying; they show, or they hide, but they always are clear, for they always speak the transparent mystery, the mystery of transparence. Thus all commentary is ponderous and uselessly verbose—all the more so if it employs the narrative mode, and expands the mysterious story intelligently into explanatory episodes which in turn imply a fleeting clarity. If Ovid, perhaps prolonging a tradition, introduces into the fable of Narcissus the fate—which one might call telling—of the nymph Echo, it is surely in order to tempt us to discover there a lesson about language which we ourselves add, after the fact. Nevertheless, the following is instructive: since it is said that Echo loves Narcissus by staying out of sight, we might suppose that Narcissus is summoned to encounter a voice without body, a voice condemned always to repeat the last word and nothing else—a sort of nondialogue: not the language whence the Other would have approached him, but only the mimetic, rhyming alliteration of a semblance of language. Narcissus is said to be solitary, but it is not because he is excessively present to himself; it is rather because he lacks, by decree (you shall not see yourself), that reflected presence—identity, the self-same—the basis upon which a living relation with life, which is other, can be ventured. He is supposed to be silent: he has no language save the repetitive sound of a voice which always says to him the self-same thing, and this is a self-sameness which he cannot attribute to himself. And this voice is narcissistic precisely in the sense that he does not love it—in the sense that it gives him nothing *other* to love. Such is the fate of the child one thinks is repeating the last words spoken, when in fact he belongs to the rustling murmur which is not language, but enchantment. And such is the fate of lovers who touch each other with words, whose contact with each other is made of words, and who can thus repeat themselves without end, marveling at the utterly banal, because their speech is not a language but an idiom they share with no other, and because each gazes at himself in the other's gaze in a redoubling which goes from mirage to admiration.

What is striking in this probably late myth, then, is that in it the prohibition upon seeing sounds once more. This taboo is a constant in the Greek tradition which remains nonetheless the domain of the visible: presence is divine merely by virtue of appearing and also in the sheer multiplicity of its appearances. There is always, however, something not to see. And this is not so much because one should not look at everything, as because—the gods being essentially visible and, indeed, the visible—it is vision that exposes men to the peril of the sacred whenever the gaze, through its arrogance quick to scrutinize and to possess, fails to look with restraint and in a retiring mode. Without calling upon Tiresias—who is too much the serviceable diviner—and leaving aside the two utterances of the oracle which might be understood as the premeditated reversal one of the other—"Know thyself," and "He will live if he does not know himself"—we ought rather to consider that Narcissus, seeing the image he does not recognize, sees in it the divine aspect, the nonliving, eternal part (for the image is incorruptible) which, without his knowing it, is his and which he does not have the right to look at, lest he fall prey to a vain desire. Thus one might say that he dies (if he dies) of being immortal, of having the immortality of appearance—the immortality which his metamorphosis into a flower attests: a funereal flower or flower of rhetoric.

◆ What is required by thought that surrenders to the multiple and seeks to avoid increasing the value of the One? "The multiple must be formed not by adding always another, higher dimension, but on the contrary, very simply, with great sobriety, at the level of readily available dimensions: always $n - 1$. The one participates in the multiple by always being subtracted." (Deleuze-Guattari.) Whence the possible conclusion that the one is, in that case, no longer one, but the fraction less by which the multiple multiplies itself (thereby constituting itself as multiple), without, however, unity's being inscribed in multiplicity as lack. This is the most difficult point. And is it not a matter, actually, of a normative model's being imposed under the auspices of a particular type of knowledge?

The multiple is ambiguous. At first, its ambiguity seems easy to account for: from a certain multiplicity—from the varied, the changing, or the diverse—unitary totality is formed (by the smoothly continuous steps of dialectical or practical reason, or indeed by the appeal of mystical reconciliation). This totality preserves by altering multiplicity; it preserves diversity and variation as means or as mediating moments. Or, mystically, by casting them into the great fire where they are consumed, or confused one in the other. But then multiple, varied, or separate things, falling under the fascination of the One, have only served unity as vehicles or as perceptible figures or as proxies. They are means of approaching what cannot be near in any other way; they are the delay and the instrument of fulfillment in the uni-verse which is to be realized, or feigned. From the unity of the individual subject (be it a fissured subject, always double, vainly desiring), to the universal, supreme One, the multiple, the different will only ever have been a moment of transition: reflections of the great Presence which, even bearing no name, is consecrated on high. Such a bold mixture of dialectic and of sheer (mystical) elevation through the hope of salvation must not be underestimated, for at stake in it is what all moral thinking and all intellectual disciplines (until today, or yesterday) have aimed for.

Still, the law of the One with its glorious, inexorable-inaccessible primacy, excludes the multiple *as* multiple. And even if this be by way of long detours, it guides the other back toward the same, substituting things that are different for difference, without letting the latter so much as enter the question, so powerful and necessary is the language program that answers for the order of a habitable universe (where we are promised that everything will be—that everything is, thus, already—present, and partaking of the graspable-ungraspable Presence). But this sovereignty of the One and the Same—mysterious or simple (at hand or hoped for), dominating everything in

advance and reigning over every being as over being itself, drawing
into its orbit all appearances as well as all essences, and everything
that can be said as well as all that remains to be said (formulations,
fictions, questions, answers, propositions of truth and of error,
affirmations, negations, images, symbols, words of life and of
death)—indicates precisely that outside of the sovereignty of the
One and of the Whole, outside of the Universe and also of its
beyond, and when all is accomplished (when death finally comes, in
the form of a life fulfilled), the demand without any rights, the demand of the other (the multiple, the impoverished, the lost) presses
as never before, as that which has always escaped realization. And
thus, for thought which has reached its culmination—for thought
whose completion has put it to sleep—the wakeful and incessant
obsession with others is affirmed. The affirmation is void, and the
obsession is with others in their un-presence. Moreover, thought
does not know how to acknowledge this obsession. But it knows
that this nocturnal disaster is thought's due and is conferred upon
thought in order that thought might be assigned a disjointed perpetuity. Such are perhaps the premises of writing—of the overwhelming overturning of writing, inasmuch, in any case, as it is over.

◆ The attraction of the simple lies in its being the gift—never
given—of the One: Of the whole which we know only as fully deployed, and in whose retreat the "one and only time," the infinite
wealth of the first and last time is hidden away, mortifying itself in
the folds of the reserve that safeguards it.[21] It is thus that we are always authorized to say, the simple is not simple, without being led
by this formula to say anything that does not still protect the inaccessibility of the One, its separation from being, its fascinating
transcendence. The complex, as distinct from the simple, is the
more or less hierarchical entanglement that lends itself to analysis
for the purpose of being sorted out and also maintained as one
whole. And the multiple too, can easily be reduced, inasmuch as it
is constructed by all the numbers up to the plus sign indicating yet

one more: at least, this is the case as long as the unit is the constitutive agent, in collaboration with the immovable One. But the multiple *as* multiple refers us to the *Als-Struktur,* the structure of the *as*: to a plurality removed from unity, and from which unity is always removed; to a relation not ours but the other's, and which is a relation because of the other who is not *one,* or unified. Or again, the *Als-Struktur* introduces us to difference, not to be confused with the different, to the fragmentary without fragments, to the *remainder*: that which is left to be written and which, like the disaster, has always preceded, and ruined, all beginnings, including the beginning of writing and of language. (And yet, the structure of the *as*—the multiple as multiple, *as such* or in itself—tends to reestablish the identity of the nonidentical, the unity of the not-one, attenuating detachment and stabilizing it in a form; the thought of the multiple is once more deferred, and thereby it keeps in relation with the impermanence of difference which does not lend itself to thought, or submit.)

◆ *"Sovereignty is NOTHING."* Pronounced thus the word "nothing" does not only imply the ruin of sovereignty, for sovereign ruin could still be a way for Sovereignty to affirm itself by elevating and glorifying nothingness. Sovereignty, always on the lookout for such possibilities—in accordance with the schema of negativity—would deploy itself absolutely, then, in that which would tend to deny it absolutely. But it may be that nothing is not at work here. Perhaps, in its ostentatiously trenchant form, it only hides what is hidden in what cannot be named, the neutral—the neutral which always neutralizes itself and which has about it nothing sovereign that has not already surrendered in advance: either by subsiding into the imprecision of the One, or by way of the negative rhythm of the other, the negation which neither denies nor affirms but which, with the infinite erosion of repetition, lets the Other be marked and unmarked and remarked as that which has no relation with anything that can be present, or absent.

◆ *"But no, always*
   Spreading the wing of the impossible
   You wake, with a cry,
   From the site, which is only a dream . . . " (Yves Bonnefoy.)

◆ An isolated sentence—aphoristic, not fragmentary—tends to
reverberate like an oracular utterance having the self-sufficiency of
a communication to which nothing need be added. If we isolate
this sentence of Wittgenstein's, which I cite from memory (memory singularizes), "Philosophy combats reason's enchantment (its
ravishment) by language," it strikes us rather forcefully as, in a
way, obvious: the point would be to arrive at a "pure" reason by
preserving it from the fascination of a certain language—"literary"
language, probably; or, indeed, "philosophical." But how should
such a combat be pursued? By means of language, once again; and
as soon as the hope expressed in the *Tractatus* is renounced, it becomes a matter of a struggle waged by language against itself. This
would restore the conditions of the dialectic, unless one were seeking an exact or true language to be evaluated by simple, silent
reason—by ideal reason, which is liable immediately to be accused
of wielding a hidden violence. For, judge of all judgments, authority on all knowledge and power, it appears to reduce language to a
featureless terrain across which truth would be transmitted without
being in any way affected. As if, precisely, reason spoke without
speaking. This can—*à la rigueur*—be affirmed, but in a sense
which is not strictly reasonable. Whence the contradictions that
straightaway impede. We may well suspect that the neutral is in
play in the infiniteness of language, but the neutral does not have
the property of giving neutrality to language as a characteristic, for
it is ungraspable, except at infinity, and as soon as it is grasped. It
is always ready, as a negative question, to fall either toward the
One or toward the Other, which it retains, repetitively, by its retreat. The neutral is thus in relation with the infiniteness of language, which no totality can ever close and which is affirmed—if

ever it is—outside of the affirmation and of the negation that established knowledge and usage make familiar to us. Whence the obligation not to speak *on* language without bearing in mind that one is confining oneself to the limitations of a particular body of knowledge, but rather to speak *on the basis of* language, which is precisely not a basis, except inasmuch as it is the unspeakable demand which nevertheless is that of speaking.

Still, Wittgenstein's sentence has not, for all this, been disqualified. It remains, saying, perhaps—as I believe someone has stated—that the great audacity of thought consists in daring to be sober: in not allowing the melodramatic to intoxicate it—the enchantment of profundity, the spell of the essential. This is important, but only provided one remember the other peril at the same time: the tempting rigor of order. Then philosophy would be the battle of reason against the reasonable as well.

♦ "The blue of the sky" is what best expresses the sky's emptiness: *the disaster as withdrawal outside the sidereal abode, and as refusal of nature's sacredness.*

♦ Confident of language—of language understood as the defiant challenge which has been confided to us, just as we have been entrusted to it.

♦ To keep the secret is evidently to tell it as a nonsecret, inasmuch as it is not tellable.

♦ The isolated, aphoristic sentence is attractive because it affirms definitively, as if nothing besides this sentence spoke anymore in its vicinity. The allusive sentence, also isolated—speaking, not speaking (effacing what it says at the same time that is speaks)—makes ambiguity a positive value. "Let us consider I have not spoken." The first sentence is normative; the second thinks it escapes the illusion of truth, but it succumbs to illusion itself as truth, and believes that what has been written can be kept back. The demand of the fragmentary is exposure to these two kinds of risk: brevity does not satisfy it; in the margins or the background of a supposedly complete discourse, it reiterates this briefness in snatches and, in the mirage of the return, knows not whether it is not giving a new assurance to that which it extracts from certainty. Let us heed this warning: "There is reason to fear that, like ellipsis, the fragment—the 'I say practically nothing and take it back right away'—makes mastery over all that goes unsaid possible, arranging in advance for all the continuities and supplements to come." (Jacques Derrida.)

◆ The question that is always to be questioned: "Does the multiple amount, finally, to just two?" One answer: whoever says two, only *repeats* One (or dual unity), unless the second term—inasmuch as it is the Other—is infinitely multiple. Or unless the repetition of One maintains only to dissipate unity (perhaps fictively). Thus there are not two discourses: there is discourse—and then there would be dis-course, were it not that of it we "know" practically nothing. We "know" that it escapes systems, order, possibility, including the possibility of language, and that writing, perhaps—writing, where totality has let itself be exceeded—puts it in play.

◆ The water in which Narcissus sees what he shouldn't is not a mirror, capable of producing a distinct and definite image. What he sees is the invisible in the visible—in the picture the undepicted, the unstable unknown of a representation without presence, which reflects no model: he sees the nameless one whom only the name he does not have could hold at a distance. It is madness he sees, and death. (But *for* us, us who name Narcissus, and establish him as a doubled Same—as containing, that is to say, unknowingly, and knowing full well, the Other within the same, death in life. For us, what Narcissus sees is the essence of the secret: a schism which in fact is no schism, and which would give him a divided self without any I, while also depriving him of all relation to others.) The glistening of the spring shows something clear—the attractive image of someone—yet at the same time blurring this clarity limpidly, it prevents the stable fixity of sheer visibility (which could be appropriated), and drags everything—he who is called upon to see and what it is he believes he sees—into a confusion of desire and fear (terms which hide the hidden, a death which would not be death). Lacoue-Labarthe, in very precious reflections, reminds us of what Schlegel is supposed to have said: "Every poet is Narcissus." We should not be content simply to rediscover in this statement the superficial mark of a certain romanticism according to which creation—poetry—is absolute subjectivity and the poet a living subject in the poem that reflects him, just as he is a poet by virtue of having transformed his life into poetry by incarnating in it his pure subjectivity. One ought, no doubt, to understand Schlegel's statement in another way too: in the poem, where the poet writes himself, he does not recognize himself, for he does not become conscious of himself. He is excluded from the facile, humanistic hope that by writing, or "creating," he would transform his dark experience into greater consciousness. On the contrary: dismissed, excluded from what is written—unable even to be present by virtue of the nonpresence of his very death—he has to renounce all conceivable relations of a self (either living or dying) to the poem which henceforth belongs to the other, or else will remain without any belonging at all. The poet is Narcissus to the extent that Narcissus is an anti-Narcissus: he who, turned away from himself—causing the detour of which he is the effect, dying of not re-cognizing himself—leaves the trace of what has not occurred.

◆ These are the words of Ovid on Narcissus that should be retained: *"He perishes by his eyes"* (by seeing himself as a god—which recalls: Whoever sees God dies). And these, too: *"Unhappy, because you were not the other, because you were the other."* Why unhappy? The unhappiness is that of missing origins and infertility; it comes of having neither forebears not descendants. Unhappy is the sterile orphan, the image of solitary misfortune. Other without being other. This provides for dialectical developments or, on the contrary, fixes in motionless exactitude, from which poetry is not excluded.

◆ To live without a lifetime—likewise, to die forsaken by death.
. . . To write elicits such enigmatic propositions.

◆ It is language that is "cryptic": not only as a totality that is exceeded and untheorizable, but inasmuch as it contains pockets,
cavernous places where words become things, where the inside is out
and thus inaccessible to any cryptanalysis whatever—for deciphering is required to keep the secret secret. The code no longer suffices.
The translation is infinite. And yet we have to find the key word that
opens and does not open. At that juncture something gets away safe-
ly, something which frees loss and refuses the gift of it. *"'I' can only
save an inner self by placing it in 'me,'* separate from myself, *outside."*
(Derrida.) This is a sentence with unlimited developments. But
when the other of I—the "me"—appropriates word-things in order
to bury a secret in them and to enjoy it without joy, in the fear and
the hope that it be communicated (shared in common with someone
else in the lack of any common measure between them), then it is a
petrified language that lends itself, through which nothing can be
transmitted, not even that there is something untransmittable. It is
perhaps in this direction that "the idiom of desire" tends, with its
mimetic motivations whose sum is unmotivated and which offer
themselves to decipherment as the indecipherable absolute.
Granted, the desire to write—which writing carries off and which
carries writing along—does not persist as a phenomenon to which
the general term "desire" could be applied, but refracts into a multi-
tude of hidden or deceptively manifest desires producing the effect
of nonarbitrariness in a variety of ways (anagram, rhythm, interior
rhyme, magical play of letters); and this effect makes of the most
"reasonable" language a contaminated process, rich in what it cannot say, inappropriate for what it does say, and stating in secret
(well or ill kept) the indefinable impropriety.
   To write without desiring to and without intending to: what is it
that hides here? What hides, not simply in the return of the undesirable and involuntary, but here? It is too easy to answer: the patience

to write—patience that persists all the way to writing's most extreme passivity (no automatic writing has been able to do this). The desire to die is likewise discernible here—but too easily—in the collision that divides here: to write without desire, to desire to write no longer—each is extinguished and reignited by the other in a perpetuity which seems to outdo time, or at least to change it, so that the disaster, the instability of the disaster, cannot exhaust its decline.

◆ *"To keep a secret— to refrain from saying some particular thing—presupposes that one could say it. This is nothing remarkable: it is merely a rather unpleasant kind of restraint. —Even so, it does relate to the question of the secret in general: to the fact (it is no fact) of wondering whether the secret is not linked to there being still something left to say when all is said; it does suggest Saying (with its glorious capital), always in excess of everything said. —The not-apparent in the whole when it is totally manifest; that which withdraws, hides in the demand that all be disclosed: the dark of the clearing or the error of truth itself. —The un-knowledge after absolute knowledge which does not, precisely, allow us to conceive of any 'after.' —Except as introduced by the imperative of the return, which 'designifies' every before, as well as every afterward, by untying them from the present, rendering them foreign to every tense. —The secret escapes; it is never circumscribed; it makes itself boundless. What is hidden in it is the necessity of being hidden. —There is nothing secret, anywhere; this is what the secret always says. —All the while not saying it. For, with the words 'there is' and 'nothing,' the enigma continues to rule, preventing installation and repose. —The stratagem of the secret is either to show itself, to make itself so visible that it isn't seen (to disappear, that is, as a secret), or to hint that the secret is only secret where there is no secret, or no appearance of any secret. —The secret is not linked to an 'I,' but to the curve of the space which cannot be called intersubjective, for the I-subject is related to the Other inasmuch as the Other is not a subject, and in the inequality of difference, in the absence of community, by virtue of the un-common of communication. —'He will live henceforth in the secret': has this disquieting sentence been elucidated?*

—It is as though it were said that for him death would occur in life. —Let us leave to silence this sentence which only means, perhaps, silence."

◆ I inquire into this affirmation, which is not to be neglected or treated lightly: "The ethics of revolt is opposed to all classical notions of the Sovereign Good, and to all moral or immoral claims, for it constructs, protects, maintains an empty place, letting another history come to us." (Guy Lardreau, Christian Jambet.) An initial remark: revolt, yes, if revolt is understood as the demand of a turning point where time changes, where the extreme of patience is linked in a relation with the extreme of responsibility. But one cannot, then, assimilate revolt and rebellion. Rebellion only reintroduces war, which is to say the struggle for mastery and domination. This does not mean that one should not struggle against the master with the instruments of his mastery; but it means that at the same time it is right to appeal, helplessly, to "the infinitely multiplied distortion" where mastery and desire, exerting their absolute reign, collide without knowing it (precisely because they know, and only know, all) with the multiple other, the other multiplicity, that never is resolved into one. And what about the *other* history, if its characteristic trait is not to be a history—not in the sense of *Historie,* or in the sense of *Geschichte* (which implies the idea of unification)? What about the *other* history, wherein nothing of the present ever happens, which no event or advent measures or articulates? Foreign to the succession of moments, which is linear even when it is hindered and as zigzagging as it is dialectical, the other history is the deployment of a plurality which is not that of the world or of numbers. It is a history in excess, a "secret," separate history, which presupposes the end of visible history, though it denies itself the very idea of beginning and of end. It is always in relation with an unknown that requires the utopia of total knowledge because it exceeds this utopia—an unknown which is not linked to the irrational beyond reason or even to an irrationality proper to reason, but which is perhaps the return to an *other* meaning in the laborious work of "designification." The *other* history would be a feigned history, which is not to say that it is a mere nothing, but that it is always calling forth the void of a nonplace, the gap that it is, and that separates it from itself. It is unbelievable because any belief in it would have to overlook it.

◆ Memorial: to speak of Wittgenstein (for example) is to speak of a person who remains unknown. He did not wish — as a philosopher — to be one, nor did he wish to be known, any more than he taught out of choice; likewise, the majority of his published works is unauthorized. Whence — perhaps — the fact that so many of his investigations are fragmentary, opening onto the fragmentary. He cannot be considered a destroyer. To question is always to transgress, and the simplicity of such overwhelmingly bold thought is always that of respect, respect for thought, rejection of pathos. If Wittgenstein gives the impression of being on the outskirts of the history of philosophy, he gives one the feeling not just that he is alone and isolated — no one is — but that there is a nonhistorical history of something which can only be called thought.

◆ He who waits does not, precisely, await *you*. It is thus that you are, however, awaited, but not in the vocative mode: not called.

◆ Why one God? Why is One somehow above God, the God who has a pronounceable name? One is obviously not a number; "one" is not the opposite of "several": between monotheism and polytheism, there is no significant difference. Zero is not a number either, any more than it is an absence of numbers; nor is it a concept. Perhaps the "One" is meant to preserve "God" from every qualifying term, such as "good," and especially "divine." The "One" is what least authorizes union, even with the infinitely distant; still less does it authorize mystical elevation and fusion. The rigorous exactitude and the impossibility of the One (which is not unity) do not even allow for transcendence as its essential orientation. It has no horizon: it does not have the horizon for its meaning. The One is not even unique; it is no more unique than it is singular. The great effect it has upon thought comes from its removal from all forms of dialectic and from every thought process. To think is to approach the thought of the One which strictly escapes thought, even though thought is turned toward the One as the needle of the compass toward the pole which it does not indicate — turned? Turned aside, rather. The strictness of the One which prescribes nothing, evokes that in the Law which law cannot decree: that which is superior to all prescriptions, and so high that there is no height at which it reveals itself. The Law, with the authority above all the justifications that tend to be attributed to it (so that it hardly matters whether it is legitimate or not), is already a lowering of the One which, neither high nor low, neither unique nor secondary, freely admits of all the equivalences which leave it intact: the Same, the Simple, Presence. But one can also say that the One, more than simply allowing these equivalences, requires all the notions of opposition that are adverse to it, for they violate only the better thereby to acknowledge it. When we feel the need to think coherently, or when we are ill at ease because we cannot unify our knowledge, is it only because of the ordinary standard of unity, or is it not rather on account of a forgotten reverence for the One without any referent, which we sense unmistakably every time we encounter translations of it — ethical or not — such as the Superego, or even the transcendental "I"? What would happen if the One could be defeated? How could it be defeated? Perhaps by speaking, by a certain kind of utterance. Such is probably the combat of the disaster. Was it, in a way, Kafka's combat, who fought for the One against the One?

♦ Hölderlin: *"Whence comes, then, among men the sickly desire that there be only the one, and that there be nothing but is part of the one?"*

♦ Combat of passivity, combat which reduces itself to naught — to extreme patience — combat which the neutral does not succeed in indicating. Combat in order not to name the combat. Its substance, or the unimaginable reality of it, exceeds reference, as does the One, and this constitutes no dualism, for how could one enter into an account, or introduce into the interval of a discourse, that which is given as the exclusion of the conditions of its being given, or as its *a priori* interruption?

♦ What Kafka gives us — the gift we do not receive — is a sort of combat through literature for literature: a struggle which is — and is at the same time escaped by — its aim. It is so different from what we know by the name "combat" or by any other name, that even the term "unknown" does not suffice to make it perceptible to us, since it is as familiar as it is strange to us. "Bartleby the Scrivener" belongs to the same combat, inasmuch as his "preference not to" has none of the simplicity of a refusal.

♦ *"To acknowledge how literature acts upon men — this is perhaps the ultimate wisdom of the West; perhaps in this wisdom the people of the Bible will recognize itself."* (Levinas.)

♦ It is strange that K. should have been considered by so many commentators bound for madness at the end of *The Castle.* From the start he is outside of the opposition reason-madness, for everything he does is without any relation whatever to the reasonable, and yet absolutely necessary: that is to say, correct, or justified. Likewise, it does not seem possible that he should die (either damned or saved — this is of little importance). For one thing, it isn't living and dying that are at stake in his combat. But then too, he is too tired (his fatigue is indeed the one trait which is accentuated as the narrative unfolds) — too tired to die. Too tired for the coming of his death not to change into an interminable nonarrival.

♦ Jewish messianic thought (according to certain commentators), suggests the relation between the event and its nonoccurrence. If the Messiah is at the gates of Rome among the beggars and lepers, one might think that his incognito protects or prevents him from coming, but, precisely, he is recognized: someone, obsessed with questioning and unable to leave off, asks him: "When will you come?"

His being there is, then, not the coming. With the Messiah, who is there, the call must always resound: "Come, Come." His presence is no guarantee. Both future and past (it is said at least once that the Messiah has already come), his coming does not correspond to any presence at all. Nor does the call suffice. There are conditions — the efforts of men, their virtue, their repentance — which are known; there are always other conditions which are not. And if it happens that to the question "When will you come?" the Messiah answers, "Today," the answer is certainly impressive: so, it is today! It is now and always now. There is no need to wait, although to wait is an obligation. And when is it now? When is the now which does not belong to ordinary time, which necessarily overturns it, does not maintain but destabilizes it? When? — especially if one remembers that this "now" which belongs to no text, but is the now of a severe, fictitious narrative, refers to texts that make it once more dependent upon realizable-unrealizable conditions: "Now, it only you heed me, or if you are willing to listen to my voice." Finally, the Messiah — quite the opposite in this respect, from the Christian hypostasis — is by no means divine. He is a comforter, the most just of the just, but it is not even sure that he is a person — that he is someone in particular. When one commentator says, The Messiah is perhaps I, he is not exalting himself. Anyone might be the Messiah — must be he, is not he. For it would be wrong to speak of the Messiah in Hegelian language — "the absolute intimacy of absolute exteriority" — all the more so because the coming of the Messiah does not yet signify the end of history, the suppression of time. It announces a time more future, as the following mysterious text conveys, than any prophesy could ever foretell: "All prophets — there is no exception — have prophesied only for the messianic time [*l'epokhe?*].[22] As for future time, what eye has seen it except Yours, Lord, who will act for him who is faithful to you and keeps waiting." (Levinas and Scholem.)

♦ Why did Christianity need a Messiah who was God? It does not suffice to say: because of impatience. But if we make historical figures divine, it is surely through a hasty subterfuge. And why the idea of the Messiah? Why the necessity of a just finish? Why can we not bear, why do we not desire that which is without end? The messianic hope—hope which is dread as well—is inevitable when history appears politically only as an arbitrary hubbub, a process deprived of meaning or direction. But if political thinking becomes messianic in its turn, this confusion, which removes the seriousness from the search for reason (intelligibility) in history—and also from the requirement of messianic thought (the realization of morality)—simply attests to a time so frightful, so dangerous, that any recourse appears justified: can one maintain any distance at all when Auschwitz happens? How is it possible to say: Auschwitz has happened?

◆ As the German expression has it, the last judgment is the youngest day, and it is a day surpassing all days. Not that judgment is reserved for the end of time. On the contrary, justice won't wait; it is to be done at every instant, to be realized all the time, and studied also (it is to be learned). Every just act (are there any?) makes of its day the last day or—as Kafka said—the very last: a day no longer situated in the ordinary succession of days but one that makes of the most commonplace ordinary, the extraordinary. He who has been the contemporary of the camps is forever a survivor: death will not make him die.

◆ The substitution of rules for law in modern times seems an attempt not only to demystify power's link to prohibition, but also to free thought from the One by proposing, to everyday human affairs, the multiplicity of undetermined possibilities created by technologies. But there has always been an ambiguity in what goes by the name of law: in its sacred, sovereign guise, it claims to derive from nature; it annexes to itself the noble prestige of the blood; it is not power but omnipotence. There is nothing but the law: whatever it is exerted against, is simply nothing: not humanity, but only myths, monsters, fascinations. Judaic law is not sacred, but holy. In place of nature—which it does not invest with the magic of sin—it puts relations, choices, mandates: that is to say, a language of obligations. In place of the ethnic, it puts the ethical. Rites are religious, but they do not transform the everyday into religious affectivity; they seek, rather, to lighten the time that has no history by knitting it together through practices, services—by forming a meticulous network of consents in the glad daylight of historical memories and anticipations. There remains judgment. It is left for the highest: God alone judges, which is again to say, the One. The One which liberates. For there is no heaven where it can reign, nor any measure by which it can be measured, nor any thought which can lower it to a level at which it would be thinkable at all. Whence the temptation to think of the One as dissolved into absence, or as returning in the inexorability of the Law, which is not a practice so much as sheer, intimidating authority, and which comes less from study than from fascinated, reverential reading. Saint Paul wanted to emancipate us from the Law: the Law enters into the drama of the sacred, the sacred tragedy, life born of death and inseparable from it.

◆ Laws—prosaic laws—free us, perhaps, from the Law by substituting for the invisible majesty of time the various constraints of space. Similarly, rules suppress, in the term "law," what power—ever primary—evokes. Rules also suppress the rights which go along with the notion of law, and establish the reign of pure procedure which—a manifestation of technical competence, of sheer knowledge—invests everything, controls everything, submits every gesture to its administration, so that there is no longer any possibility of liberation, for one can no longer speak of oppression. Kafka's trial can be interpreted as a tangle of three different realms (the Law, laws, rules). This interpretation, however, is inadequate, because to justify it one would have to assume a fourth realm not derived from the other three—the overarching realm of literature itself. But literature rejects this dominant point of view, all the while refusing to be dependent upon, or symbolized by, any other order at all (such as pure intelligibility).

♦ In "Bartleby," the enigma comes from "pure"writing, which can only be that of a copyist (rewriting). The enigma comes from the passivity into which this activity (writing) disappears, and which *passes* imperceptibly and suddenly from ordinary passivity (reproduction), to the beyond of all passiveness: to a life so passive — for it has the hidden decency of dying — that it does not have death for an ultimate escape, nor does it make death an escape. Bartleby copies; he writes incessantly, and cannot stop long enough to submit to anything resembling control. *I would prefer not to.* This sentence speaks in the intimacy of our nights: negative preference, the negation that effaces preference and is effaced therein: the neutrality of that which is not among the things there are to do — the restraint, the gentleness that cannot be called obstinate, and that outdoes obstinacy with those few words. . . . Language, perpetuating itself, keeps still.

♦ *Learn to think with pain.*

♦ Thought seems immediate (I think, I am), and yet it is related to study: one has to rise early to think; one has to think and never be sure of thinking. We are not sufficiently awake. We have to wake beyond wakefulness; then vigilance is the night, wakeful. It is pain, and separates, but not visibly (not by a dislocation or a disjunction that would be spectacular): silently, quieting the noise behind words. Perpetual pain, lost, forgotten. It does not make thought painful. It does not let itself be comforted. The pensive smile of an inscrutable face which heaven and earth — both vanished — and day, night — each having passed into the other — leave to him who no longer looks and who, bound to return, will never leave.

♦ The written word: in it we no longer live. Not that it announces: "Yesterday it was over." But it is our discord, the gift of the word which is precarious.

◆ Let us share eternity in order to make it transitory.

◆ *What remains to be said.*

◆ *Shining solitude, the void of the sky, a deferred death: disaster.*

Notes

1. *L'Arrêt de mort* (Paris: Gallimard, 1948), trans. Lydia Davis under the title *Death Sentence* (Barrytown, N.Y.: Station Hill Press, 1978).
2. This definition recalls Heidegger's *alèthéia,* in "The Origin of the Work of Art," for example. In *The Writing of the Disaster,* Blanchot ponders the word *alèthéia,* its possible etymologies and meaning.
3. Michel Foucault, in "La Pensée du dehors," *Critique,* no. 229 (June 1966), was the first to emphasize the interiorlessness of Blanchot's writing, and the implications of his term *le dehors.*
4. *L'Espace littéraire* (Paris: Gallimard, 1955), trans. Ann Smock as *The Space of Literature* (Lincoln: University of Nebraska Press, 1982). Readers approaching Blanchot for the first time might wish to look at the general introduction to his work provided as a preface to the 1982 translation.
5. *L'Entretien infini* (Paris: Gallimard, 1969).

1. "Not so much what we undergo, as that which goes under" is my translation for *le subissement,* the word Blanchot supplies lest we misunderstand the word "suffering" (*souffrance*), and which he forms from *subir* ("to undergo, to suffer"). Blanchot writes: " 'Est-ce que tu as souffert pour la connaissance?' Cela nous est demandé par Nietzsche, à condition que nous ne nous méprenions pas sur le mot souffrance: *le subissement,* le 'pas' du tout à fait passif en retrait par rapport à toute vue, tout connaître." —Tr.

2. Simone Weil. —Tr.

3. The French word I have translated as "title" is *surnom*, which Blanchot hyphenates, *sur-nom*, thus emphasizing the prefix, which recurs in *survie*, "survival." —Tr.

4. "The uneventfulness of the neutral wherein the lines not traced retreat" is my elaboration upon Blanchot's expression *"le désoeuvrement du neutre."* *Le désoeuvrement* is a word Blanchot has long used in close association with *l'oeuvre* (the work of art, of literature). It means the work as the work's lack—the work as unmindful of being or not being, as neither present nor absent: neutral. It also means idleness, inertia. My word "uneventfulness" tries to express this idea of inaction, of nothing's happening, and my additional phrase "the lines not traced retreat," recalling an earlier expression in this book, "the retreat of what never has been treated," seeks to retain the relation which this fragment is evoking and which is, so to speak, spelled out in the word *désoeuvrement*: the relation between the work and its denial. Between writing and passivity, between being and not being a writer, being and not being the subject of the verb "to write." —Tr.

5. Blanchot writes: "Dans le rapport de moi (le même) à Autrui. . . ." Thus he makes explicit that the relation of self to others (of subject to the Other) is also the relation of identity to otherness, or of sameness to difference. He is able to suggest this implicitly in many other passages because the expression for "myself" is *moi-même* in French. When he speaks, as in the fragment following this one, of my being the same by virtue of my relation to the other ("It is through the other that I am the same"), the fact that being *myself* in French is being *moi-meme* makes the expression "I am the same" less strained than it is in English. Blanchot's sentences consistently recall that to be yourself is to be *identical: self-same*, one might say in English. But his point is always that there is no such sameness, no such identity except through the (disastrous) relation to otherness: no identity, in other words, save by virtue of its ruination. —Tr.

6. In French, "guilty" is *coupable*, and *le coup* is a blow. So innocent guilt (i.e., responsibility) is the endurance of a blow whose *-able* has been blown up: its ability to be inflicted, its ability to be borne. —Tr.

7. Blanchot's brackets. —Tr.

8. A note added subsequently, lest the ambiguity here exceed what is called for: I say "eternal philosophy" in the sense that there is in Levinas no

spectacular break with the language called "Greek," wherein the principle
of universality is preserved. But what is pronounced, or rather announced,
with Levinas is a surplus: something beyond the universal, a singularity
which can be called Jewish and which *waits* to keep on being thought.
Prophetic in this respect. Judaism, as that which exceeds all that has ever
been thought because it has ever been thought already, and which nevertheless bears the responsibility for thought yet to come: this is what *gives* us
the other philosophy of Levinas, a burden and a hope, the burden of hope.

9. Blanchot actually wrote: "[La] responsabilité . . . me donne à répon-
dre . . . de l'impossibilité d'être responsable, à laquelle cette responsabilité
sans mesure m'a toujours déjà *voué en me dévouant et me dévoyant*" (my emphasis). —Tr.

10. Blanchot writes "l'un travaillant, l'autre désoeuvrant." Tr.

11. This fragment displays several effects in French (besides the echo
passing back and forth among "turn," "overturn," "return," "detour," and
from this group to "catastrophic" and back) that are lost in my translation:
the trancelike motionlessness of the fall is called "l'immobilité d'une
mouvance"; where I say "deficiency," Blanchot writes *déception,* rhyming
with *exception*: "La déception ne laisse pass l'exception se reposer dans la
hauteur . . . l'exception échappe, la déception dérobe."—Tr.

12. "In answer to the entreaty which strips and flays me and destroys
my ability to answer" is my translation of "dans la supplique d'un supplice
infini." *La supplique* is "supplication," *le supplice* is "torture."—Tr.

13. Here, what Blanchot actually wrote is, "Le silence est peut-être un
mot, un mot paradoxal, le mutisme du mot (conformément au jeu de l'éty-
mologie)." I believe that the etymology referred to is that of the expression
Motus! ("Silence! Not a word!"), a latinization of the word *mot* ("word").
Motus, meaning "not a word," is said to have developed from the expression
ne dire mot ("to say nothing"), an expression similar to others such as *n'y voir
goutte* ("to see nothing"). —Tr.

14. "It has the suddenness of the interminable torment which is always
over already" is my expansion upon "à la fois subit (subi) et patient. . . ."
Subit is 'sudden"; *subi* is "suffered," suffered as the suffering Blanchot calls
subissement. This suffering goes under suddenly, *and* is undergone patiently. —Tr.

15. Makes the *coup coup-able.* See note 6, page 22. —Tr.

16. René Char. —Tr.

17. "Trip": *achopper*; "elude": *échapper*. "La philosophie qui met tout en question, achoppe à la poésie qui est la question qui lui échappe." —Tr.

18. Georges Bataille. —Tr.

19. As is well known, and as I have noted in *L'Entrien infini*, rhythm, according to Benveniste, probably does not derive from *rheô*, but, through *rhutmos*, from *rhusmos*, which Benveniste defines as "changing, fluid configuration."

20. The reference is to Roland Barthes and his *Fragments d'un discours amoureux* (Paris: Seuil, 1977), trans. Richard Howard as *A Lover's Discourse: Fragments* (New York: Hill and Wang, 1978). —Tr.

21. In Blanchot's phrase, which I have translated rather freely, the word for "fold," *pli*, not only resounds in the word *déplié* ("deployed" in my version) and *repliement* (my "retreat"), but is echoed in the word I have rendered as "mortify": *supplicier*. Blanchot writes: ". . . l'ensemble que nous ne connaissons que comme déplié et dont le repliement dérobe l'infinie richesse de 'l'une seule fois' qui s'y suplicie." —Tr.

22. Blanchot's brackets. —Tr.

Agacinski, Sylviane, 35, 47
Antelme, Robert, 83
Archilochus, 5
Aristotle, 80, 102
Arnim, Bettina von, 112

Barl-Shem, 121
Barthes, Roland, 119, 150
Bataille, Georges, 88, 90, 109–10, 150
Baudelaire, Charles, 32
Benveniste, Emile, 94, 150
Berger, Joseph, 83
Bergson, Henri, 106
Blanchot, Maurice, vii–xiii; *Death Sentence*, viii, 147; *The Space of Literature*, xii, 147; *Le Très-Haut*, 17
Bonaventura, Saint, 31, 32
Bonnefoy, Yves, 132
Bopp, Franz, 107

Cantor, Georg, 104
Celan, Paul, 90–91
Char, René, 63, 113, 124, 150
Chronos, 80
Clavel, Maurice, 62

Deleuze, Gilles, 128
Derrida, Jacques, 40, 98, 134, 136
Desanti, Jean Toussaint, 103
Descartes, René, 54, 57, 103

Echo, 127

Fichte, Johann Gottlieb, 31
Foucault, Michel, 147
Freud, Sigmund, 118

Genette, Gérard, 94, 108
God, 23, 24, 26, 31, 90–92, 139, 142, 144
Goethe, Johann Wolfgang von, 119; *Sorrows of Young Werther*, 119
Guattari, Félix, 128
Guillemin, 122

Hegel, Georg Wilhelm Friedrich, 22, 40, 45, 46–47, 63, 68, 76, 92, 94, 102, 104, 108
Heidegger, Martin, 61, 94–95, 97–99, 101–2, 104, 107–10, 117, 147
Heraclitus, 77, 95

Hermogenes, 108
Himmler, Heinrich, 83
Hölderlin, Friedrich, 103, 112, 124, 140
Humboldt, Alexander von, 96, 106–7

Jabès, Edmond, 2
Jambet, Christian, 138
Job, 122

Kafka, Franz, 43, 140, 151, 143; *The
Castle*, 49, 141; *The Trial*, 53, 144
Kierkegaard, Soren, 120
Klossowski, Pierre, 57

La Rochefoucauld, François, duc de, 125
Lacoue-Labarthe, Philippe, 102, 135
Langbein, Hermann, 81, 83
Laporte, Roger, 100–101
Lardreau, Guy, 138
Leclaire, Serge, xi, 67–69
Leibniz, Gottfried Wilhelm, 64
Lenin, Vladimir, 122
Leroi-Gourhan, André, 111
Levinas, Emmanuel, xi, 18, 19, 22–25,
30, 64, 76, 77, 84, 101, 109–10, 114,
141, 142, 148–49
Lewental, Salmen, 82
Louria, Isaac, 13

M'Uzan, Michel de, 100
Mallarmé, Stéphane, 5, 7, 103, 114–15
Marx, Karl, 63, 73
Mauss, Marcel, 109
Melville, Herman, 113; *Bartleby*, xiii,
17, 141, 145

Narcissus, xi, 125–28, 134–35
Nietzsche, Friedrich, 3, 44, 76, 104–6,
109, 122–24, 147
Novalis, 8, 31, 32

Ovid, 125–27, 135

Parmenides, 102
Paul, Saint, 122, 144
Paulhan, Jean, 94, 95
Pinhas, Rabbi, 121
Pisistrates, 80
Plato, 34, 35, 54, 94–95, 102, 122;
Cratylus, 95
Pontalis, Jean Baptiste, 118
Prometheus, 5

Rilke, Rainer Marie, 117

Sade, Marquis de, 8, 45
Sartre, Jean-Paul, 22
Schelling, Friedrich Wilhelm Joseph, 99,
118
Schlegel, August W., 110
Schlegel, Friedrich, 7, 57, 60, 61, 107,
135
Schleiermacher, Friedrich, 7
Scholem, Gershom, 142
Schwarzhuber, Hans, 83
Sinclair, Isaak von, 112
Socrates, 35, 62–63, 65
Solzhenitsyn, Alexander, 81
Stalin, Josef, 83
Suson, Gilles, 80

Tiresias, 128
Todorov, Tristan, 111

Valéry, Paul, 62, 95, 107, 113

Weil, Eric, 74
Weil, Simone, 6, 147
Winnicott, Donald Woods, xi, 66, 69
Wittgenstein, Ludwig, 10, 132–33, 139

Library of Congress Cataloging-in-Publication Data
Blanchot, Maurice.
[Ecriture du désastre. English]
The writing of the disaster = L'écriture du
désastre / by Maurice Blanchot;
translated by Ann Smock.
p.   cm.
Includes bibliographical references and index.
ISBN 0-8032-6120-9
1. Blanchot, Maurice—Philosophy.
2. Literature—Philosophy.
I. Smock, Ann, 1944–   .
II. Title.   III. Title:
Ecriture du désastre.
PQ2603.L3343E2813   1995
848'.91207—dc20   94-46856   CIP

.